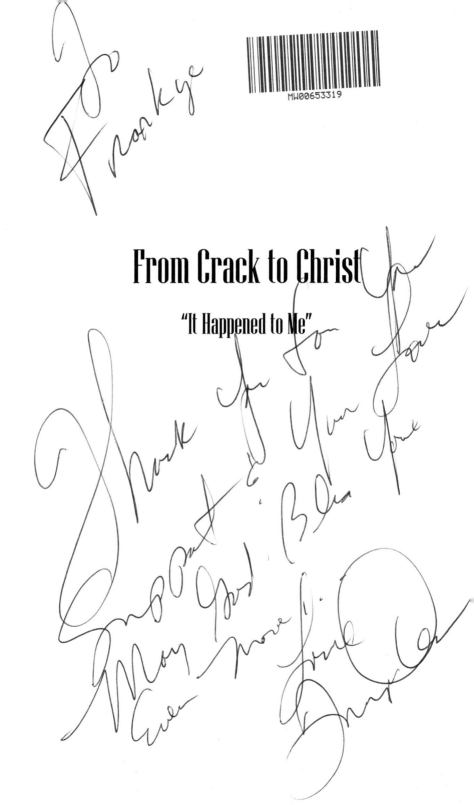

From Crack to Christ

"It Happened to Me"

From Crack to Christ

"It Happened to Me"

A True Story, written by

Tanya Davis

www.TrueVinePublishing.org

Published by True Vine Publishing Company
P.O. Box 22448, Nashville, TN. 37202
www.TrueVinePublishing.org

Cover Design: Jason Couch

Email: fromcracktochrist615@gmail.com
Website: www.fromcracktochrist.net
Facebook: www.facebook.com/fromcracktochrist
YouTube: www.youtube.com/fromcracktochrist

I gave this transcript to a few people to read. They were moved; they laughed, they cried, and they found joy in seeing deliverance. They said they were transfixed, empowered and many said they were transformed. That's when I knew this book was for everybody and it had to be published.

This is for all who have embarked upon the quest for truth about their Mother, Father, Siblings, Relatives, and Friends who have gone through drug addiction.

Questions about life and death, people and relationship, guilt and sin, forgiveness and redemption, the path to God and the road to Hell should all be answered.

Wow! This book is a must read. To understand the pain and the struggles that people face every day, trapped in a world of sin! This book will open your mind as well as reveal to you signs, so that you can be aware of any loved one that may be facing the same struggle. Reading this book rid the guilt of saying I wish I only knew or I wish that I could have done something; well now you can. This book will be your guide into the dark world of addiction without ever being there yourself and you can have the answer that's needed when trouble comes. Thank you Tanya for opening my eyes and keep changing the world by making a mark in a man's life that will never be Ease!

Love Always! Apostle Lennell D. Caldwell

What an incredible heart wrenching story by a "soldier in the army of The Lord." While I have witnessed and experienced some of Tanya's life journey; herein lies the most compelling gut-wrenching truth of "strength in the struggle" story, where so, so many never make it to the other side of safety. That is safe in the arms of Jesus! I'm so glad that we have a God, a true and living God that answers prayers. Love you forever my sister...

Evangelist Michelle D. Jackson aka (Mickey)

Tanya Davis is truly a missionary. She'd take time to come pick me up for church and make me get in the car to go get the Word. She didn't know at the time I was still using, she was trying to show me how she did it. But even during that time spent under the Word it began to convict my heart for change. When everyone turned their backs on me; she was there. "From Crack to Christ" is a true story. I experience some of life's trials and tribulations with her. I can truly say while watching her in her recovery, her life touched my life and as a result of that I'm 16 years clean and sober....

Daryl Mack, delivered addict

I met Tanya in a place where dreams are shattered and visions are lost. In a place where it seems all hope is gone. Even throughout this time she remained focused on her goals. Incarceration and separation from the outside world and the ones she loved, couldn't discourage her motivation. Tanya is truly inspiring and "From Crack to Christ" tells a story of what a true survivor is and it only gives a portion of how wonderful she is; A must read... I just want her to know I give her all the love GOD taught me how to give to a person and that's unconditional...

Laury'n West, Lethal Writing & Creative Concepts, Film, TV and Playwright

To my daughter, I'm so very proud of you. For you to share the writing in this book about your life is truly a blessing for somebody. And to the readers who are parents; the one thing you'll find in this story is "Never" give up on your children when facing devastating situations. You will see in this book that Through prayer and supplication God will turn any situation around...There's an old saying "Somebody prayed for Me" well I never stop praying for my daughter and as a result of prayer God's Love conquers all...

I Love you, Mother

This book is going to bless everyone who reads it because of the real life circumstances my mother has shared with you. I didn't know what happen, I didn't know what she went through, I knew she was on drugs once before, but I never seen that side of my mother. She's been a wonderful provider, and a hard worker, but from reading this book I now know. I am so proud of the obstacles you overcame and the mountains you had to climb. Now I'm more grateful God gave you another chance because I know firsthand what a mighty God we serve...

I love you Mommy! Parisia

To my Dear Wife, I don't know how you survived mentally after reading your book. But I do know; I'm married to a strong, amazing woman. Some things I read in your book I wanted to hurt some people. And then I wanted to cry, because I felt your pain; even now when you hurt I hurt. Just know, every day I look at you I thank God he kept you here to share the rest of your life with me... forever and always...

I Love YOU! Kenneth

PREFACE

I wrote this book so that anyone who reads it can become inspired from my trials and tribulations. I wrote this book so no one will allow life's obstacles to destroy their life; but you destroy life's obstacles. I can say with absolute confidence that Satan tried to stop me from writing this novel...But God saw fit for me to share my failures, my pain, my embarrassing moments; especially when I had to re-live some real hurtful days. I wanted to put the pencil down because of the shame I caused myself, my daughter, my family and others. But through extraordinary truths God shows his Grace and Mercy and his will for my Life; and the freedom of Addiction took place. And I owe it all to My Lord and Savior Jesus Christ... "To God be the Glory"

"I will never leave you nor forsake you..."

Hebrews 13:5

Acknowledgments

W riting this book has been an extraordinary and rewarding experience. First and foremost my deepest gratitude goes out to my mother Shirley Gene Harp and my deceased father Richard Leroy Harp, my late great grandparents Charles & Florence Davidson, my daughter Parisia Le`Marie Harp and her father Paris Lee Smith Sr.—I want to thank them for being a part of my journey that God designed for my life to be a proven testimony of God's grace and mercy. These people have shared a great part of my hardships and they never gave up on me; I will be forever grateful. I want to personally thank my forever friend Melody "Oreo" Ramsey, who saw something in me that I didn't see in myself. Who understood and wisely advised me to recovery—She was the angel God used in my life to help me recover. And my brother Thomas McIntosh always by my side and believed in me and this project. I also want to thank the late great Rev. Rufus C. Pope the most awesome Shepherd; He said I would share my story with the world, and he was right. I miss him so dearly. I also would like to thank Bishop Joseph W. Walker III who pastors me presently and through his powerful ministry I've continued to change and be inspired.

I want to thank the following people for their generous contributions during the writing of this book. Most importantly, I would like to thank my editors Jeanne Lada and Latrisha Talley for the attention to detail, advice and steadfast devotion on this project and Jason Couch an inspiring "Graphic Artist" for the beautiful cover—Who said to me, "Let's be real with the cover, it's a true story…"

My publishing company True Vine and my agent

Timothy Bond for your awesome informative and customer service, you were amazing and it was very comfortable working with you. Costawilla "Kennie" Proctor (Hair Stylist) and LaShaunna Monyette (Make-up Artist) for marketing materials. Kenneth McEastland (Photographer) for the inside "Alter Ego" photos, great job! Chris Bond for all the beautiful graphic print materials—he worked long hours on this project to make me happy. O.J. Rice Photography for my photo shoot, nice job! Thomas Staples for designing and directing my book trailer for social media promotions…Awesome Job!

I would like to thank my grandchildren Tarien Marie Harp, Taylor A`Marie Harp, and John Allon Robert Foster aka B.J. for being my motivation in life today. They keep me routed, steadfast, bound and a constant reminder why I want to continue to live and run on…

Finally, I would like to thank my husband Kenneth Thirkield, who has supported me through the course of our relationship in more ways than one. I owe him a special debt of gratitude for his support, patience, encouragement and unconditional love. *I LOVE YOU HONEY…*

Many other people, who I owe so much too, may not be mentioned by name in this story; but *I Thank You!* Because it would not have been a story at all.

 "FROM CRACK TO CHRIST"

"It happened to Me"

Also I heard the voice of the Lord saying "Whom shall I send, and who will go for us?" Then I said, "Here I am! Send me."…

Isaiah 6:8

I sometimes ponder my assignment and destiny here on earth. I envision a group of people as far as the eye can see standing before the Lord. As he issues out assignments to be carried out on Earth, he doesn't give many details, but instead speaks about an assignment which will bring much trial and tribulation. "If you will trust Me," He says, "I will bring you through in my Son's name and for my Son's sake. Then people will see my glory on your life, they will praise Me for what I have done for you and you will be blessed. Who will go for Us?"

At that moment, I see myself raise my hand and say, "Lord, I will go."

PROLOGUE

"**D**on't panic," Mama said.

"I killed her Mama, I killed her…" Her eyes were closed and she wasn't breathing. What did I do? Why did I take her with me?

I had just given birth to a beautiful baby girl, Parisia Le`Marie Harp. She had beautiful brown eyes, golden brown skin and a full head of big curly locks. We were at the house napping that evening when the phone rang. It was Dray calling, one of the guys I got high with. Boy, could he get the best dope around, "Crack" that is. He told me he had just copped. At that very moment, my addiction began stirring up inside of me to get high. I whispered, "I have my baby and no one is here to watch her, I'm not able to come right now." I hung up the phone terrified, because I wanted to take off like the *Tasmanian devil*. I couldn't help thinking to myself, *"Should I leave Parisia here alone or should I take her to the crack house with me?"* A thought followed by a muffled but unmistakable command from a voice within saying, "Go! Go!"

In an instant, I immediately packed up Parisia in a lovely pink blanket, grabbed a bottle of milk out of the refrigerator, and ran straight to my car. I grabbed hold of the wheel and in my mind I was holding even tighter to a high I was searching for with desperation. The rapture of thinking about the high consumed me for a minute or two. While driving you would have thought I was in a NASCAR race just to get to what was about to be an explosive high, one after another. Quickly, I pulled up to Dray's house. You could hear the loud sound of the brakes, and when I got out of the car you could see the skid marks on the ground, not just from the tires but from my feet, as they ran to the back of the car to get my baby. I grabbed her in one hand and my purse in the other.

Knocking relentlessly, pounding hard as I could. I thought, *"They have to be here, where is he? I could not have done all this for nothing..."* That's when the door opened. A friend of Dray's greeted me by saying, "Who you looking for?"

"I'm here to see Dray," I replied.

It was in that moment I realized the hopelessness of my situation, but when he came to the door the pipe in his hand was fired up. Dray's mouth was consumed with crack smoke and before I could say anything his lips connected with mine. He blew what was in his mouth into my mouth; it was a taste of what was coming next. My legs felt weak and shaky, and with the instincts of an addict I did the only thing that was left to do, and that was to sit Parisia in a corner and get to work.

I couldn't wait for my turn to come. The sizzle of the crack that would rush inside my head was all that mattered to me. They passed me the plate of crack that looked like precious uncut diamond stones. My hands were shaking as if I was about to praise the Lord. I loaded the pipe, flicked the lighter and inhaled deeply. As soon as Parisia began to cry, the rush hi-jacked my brain. I couldn't think. I couldn't react to the call of my baby. I took the lighter and lit it again, pulling as hard as I could to grab on to that ultimate sensation of a high. Her crying began to sound more like thunder. I heard the warning, but I was in my element and did nothing.

When I glanced around the room everyone was getting high. The smoke filled the room like a dense fog. That's when Dray told me, "Get your damn baby, and shut her ass up."

The crying was messing with their high. Others began to say

the same but in harsher words, "She's $@#%&*# up my high," someone said.

"Get your baby and leave… you can't stay here with her Tanya," Dray said.

I grabbed another one of those precious stones and flicked the lighter again and again and again, holding onto the cloud of life. It was the element that took me to a far away place where nothing on earth mattered. Still the crying was growing louder and louder and then all of a sudden…I heard nothing. What happened? Where was she? I dropped the pipe out of my hand running to her rescue. I couldn't find her. "Where is she?" I screamed. "Where is my baby?"

When I found her, her eyes wouldn't open and she wasn't breathing. I asked myself, "What have I done?" I grabbed hold of my baby in her pink blanket that now looked like the brightest shade of red. She seemed to be on fire. The paranoia high had me tripping. Now the entire place appeared to be on fire. I panicked and ran straight out the front door screaming, "My baby is dead! I killed her…"

I put her in the back seat and drove straight to the house. I knew I couldn't take her to the hospital; I was doomed to be arrested. I thought, *"Go to the house, my mother will help me."* It was only the grace and mercy of *God* that I made it to my destination. All I saw was fire on the car's tail lights, and fire on the head lights coming towards me, and when the street light changed red, I rushed through it, because it seemed to be burning too.

When I arrived at the house, my mother was sitting on the porch appearing like *God* himself. She looked like safety. If I could just get into her arms, I knew she would make everything right. Every step toward her was like 100 miles away. When I reached her, I handed her Parisia and said, "Mom I think I killed my baby…"

Whoever caused one of these little ones who believe in me to sin, it would be better for him if a millstone were hung around his neck and he was drowned in the depth of the sea. Woe to the world because of offenses! For offenses must come, but woe to that man by whom the offenses come...Mathew 18:6-8

S ome people say that a child is the product of their environment. Others say that nature is the main ingredient that determines how a child turns out. How else do you explain why children in the same family go two completely different ways? Of course, we now know that it is both nature and nurture that shapes a child. Yet, I argue that environment takes precedence. Children can overcome the deficits they are born with at birth if their environment is of a positive nature…

But what if you grew up in dual worlds? What if you had one set of adults that showed you how to "live right' and another set of adults that pulled you in another direction, into a lure of another kind of life, a life in the shadows for the fear of discovery?

Chapter One

I was born to two loving parents in 1959 in the prosperous city of Detroit, Michigan. It was the boomtown of its day, the "Paris of the Midwest," with an auto industry that had a monopoly on the world. Detroit...the city that singlehandedly created, inarguably, the most prosperous working class in the world. People had come north—Black people especially—to take advantage of Mr. Ford's generous and unparalleled offer of wages plus overtime. Mr. Ford gave people with high school diplomas or less the opportunity to purchase beautiful brick homes, attend some of the best public schools in the country and buy the same beautiful cars they were actually making themselves.

My parents, Shirley Gene and Richard Leroy Harp, had me young; they were fifteen and sixteen years old, respectively. This was a time when "Motown" was on the rise. My mother and father hung around some of the great singing legends of its time: Stevie Wonder, Smokey Robinson and The Miracles, Diana Ross and The Supremes, just to mention a few. My mother and Diana actually got into a quarrel over my father. My mother won, of course.

My mother, Shirley, had a figure that was out of this world. Her breasts were a 32 Double D, her waist a very tiny 24 inches and her hips 36 inches wide with beautiful Tina Turner legs. Diana of course was a frail skinny girl with a magnificent voice.

My father, Leroy, was a street corner singer like most. Many people back in the early '60s would form together in groups and sing. Crowds would come from everywhere and stand like they were at a concert for many hours. They would listen to the creative sounds of voices in Tenor, Bass, Soprano, and Alto. Their voices would also create the sound of the instruments. It was that sound that was so captivating and filled with love that got my mother, Shirley Gene, in trouble—now that was baby making music!

She became pregnant with me at the age of fourteen years old. Back then, when young women became pregnant they were sent down south to hide their pregnancy. Upon return the grandparents would raise the child as one of the siblings; only later would the child find out that he or she was not your sister, brother, aunt, or uncle, but your child. This had been going on for centuries. My grandparents sent my mother to Mississippi to hide birth. When she returned home, she became a loving mother and added to the love I enjoyed from my doting but strict grandparents, Charles and Florence Davidson.

We lived in a three-bedroom, one-bath house near Tireman and Joy Road on what is now known as the "Old West Side" of Detroit. The venerable Old West Side birthed some of Detroit's most prominent citizens, from revered civil rights Federal Judge Damon J. Keith, to the pioneering Detroit Congressman, George W. Crockett. In 1959, in sharp contrast to today, the Old West Side was still a thriving, vibrant community, with the requisite side-by-side barber and beauty shops, clothing stores, fruit markets and even jazz clubs. Our street was Pacific Street, dubbed "The Ocean" by the people who lived in the neighborhood.

Detroit was known for its cold weather. Every winter would be the happiest time of the year for me. The snow would fill the trees, the grass, sidewalks and the cars. The cold wind would blow, keeping everything in motion. In the morning you could hear the roaring sound of the snow plows going as early as 5 o'clock. I would wake up and look out my bedroom window to find every man and boy on the block shoveling and removing snow from the sidewalks and parking spaces. After the removal, they would save their parking spaces by putting a chair in their spot, and you dared not disrespect by removing it and pulling your car in—that would definitely stir up trouble.

Every day for me was filled with adventure. I loved building snowmen with Oreo cookies for the eyes and a long carrot for the nose. I still remember the snowball fights, which I loved. It was something about that snowball hitting you in the back of the head and feeling the cold ice sticking to your winter hat or getting inside the hood of your jacket. Oh, and I'll never forget about the angels, where you would lay in the snow and wave your arms up and down to make the wings, and your legs moving in and out would make the dress. Upon standing, you could see the print of your body as this lovely precious angel. Remember the five-color Christmas lights that would turn your tree into a multicolored vision? That must have been the precursor to the disco lighting of the '80s. My grandfather took it upon himself to fashion a bar counter top in our basement by cutting a big hole right out the center. Then cover the hole with a sheet of clear plastic covering and place the light behind it; this accommodated that disco light atmosphere. It was quite the innovative design accessory and we were—and probably still are—the only family that had that feature (my Uncle fashioned his the same way).

Rules ruled the day in the Davidson home and there were many. The rules did not allow for me to venture out like my peers. I had to be in the house by the time the street lights came on. I was not allowed to play in the alley, not allowed in the street nor could I go to the playground by myself like the other children; all of which were fascinating to me. I had to stay in front of the house or at the most, stay on the block. Eventually, as I became older I was able to do those other things, but I still had to be in the house by the time the street lights came on.

The people who lived on Pacific Street—in fact, the people who lived throughout the neighborhood—took pride in our community. This was a generation of people who believed in having a block club, community watch and the key to success was (and still is) education.

In our community my school was located near the house. I loved taking that walk to school each morning; it gave me a sense of feeling responsible and grown up. Our teachers back then paid very close attention to us and believed in disciplining the students. Yes, Whooping! From the principal, to the teachers: male and female. If you were a young girl, the male teachers wouldn't hit you on your back side, but they would take that paddle and bend your hand back a little and you received that punishment—a far cry from today's discipline.

Every spring, the flowers that our parents planted would bloom into a myriad of spring colors. Orange Daylilies, purple Crocuses, yellow Daffodils and of course, carefully tended beautiful red Roses. There wasn't any lawn service in our neighborhood either. The men in the neighborhood would share their equipment and groom the best lawns I've ever seen. This was a weekly ritual for them, while the women would carefully tend to their flowers.

Across the street lived a woman named Miss Peaches. She had been a widow since I was at least five years old. She had two children: Barbara, my age and Janet, a couple years older. They lived in a well-kept two-family flat. It was owned by a Mexican man whom we called Gus. Gus lived in the top flat and Miss Peaches lived in the bottom half. The house boasted a really wide porch that accommodated many of the children who loved to gather at this house. Miss Peaches was a woman of great character with a vibrant and shall we say curious personality. But, boy...could she cuss! It was fun hearing her say all those words that Florence and Charles Davidson wouldn't let me say. I secretly admired her vocabulary; I thought it was quite entertaining.

Miss Peaches` daughter Barbara was my best friend.

There were many, many early mornings where one of us would find ourselves waking up at the other one's house, even on Christmas Day. If I woke up at her house, Miss Peaches insisted that I, like her children, brush my teeth with Arm & Hammer baking soda. "This is better than any toothpaste selling on the market," she would tell us. We basked in her home spun wisdom, nearly as much as we enjoyed hearing her "bad words." Miss Peaches didn't miss a trick! Despite her nosiness, nearly every child in the neighborhood found themselves frequently seated on her porch. We'd gather there and talk about everything. We told Miss Peaches more than we'd tell our own mothers! *Every child needs a trustworthy adult to whom they can share things that they wouldn't tell their own parents.* That was Miss Peaches, and she never judged. She just gave you that one piece of advice you needed and some of her advice stayed with me for life.

When I was fifteen years old, I came home around three o'clock in the morning—coming back from one of our typical Friday night skating parties at the Carousel skating rink. The Carousel was located in Southwest Detroit. It was innocent entertainment (which is sadly missing today for Detroit's young people).

"I want to know why are you coming home so late, and who was that boy you were with?" queried Miss Peaches.

"Miss Peaches that was my friend, we were coming from White Castle. We went to eat after skating and after we ate, we watched the guys race their cars." I answered defensively.

Miss Peaches looked at me sternly. "Come here and sit down," she shouted. "Let me tell you this right now, don't let no boy get in your pants!"

I wondered why she was up so late, but I didn't dare ask. If Miss Peaches saw something suspicious, she wouldn't hesitate to call you or the police. It wasn't out of resentment;

you knew Miss Peaches cared dearly about you. Years later, I wish I had heeded her advice.

Then there was Mr. and Mrs. Wright, the caring grandparents on the block. The Wrights were a kind couple, and I loved them like family. They grew a garden in their backyard and shared the produce with anyone who came by or was in need. One of Pacific's families had nineteen children; Mrs. Wright gave that family a lot of her gardens' bounty. My mother would tend to their hygiene by giving them baths and doing their hair. Grandmother would cook and invite them to have supper, or prepare large plates for them that included all the fixings to take home with them. In fact, the whole neighborhood rushed to envelop this family, almost like the blood that rushes to a new wound so that a scab can develop that protects it.

Also neighbors were Mr. and Mrs. Scott, my grand-parents' closest friends. They did everything together. Mr. Scott, whom we loved, referred to as "Scotty". He and my grandfather would hang for hours every day after work. The one thing I remember most about them was that they had a huge fire arm collection. Between them both they had riffles, hand guns and plenty of bullets. They would shoot off the back top porches like they were at a gun range, and other times take it upon themselves to single-handedly capture criminals in the neighborhood; who were trying to break into someone's house or car. This was considered to be their small act of kindness.

"Boss I got one to go…call the police," Scotty would say to my Grandfather.

I called my grandfather, "Granddaddy"—he was a good man. He was a supervisor at Herman Keifer Hospital, one of Detroit's medical facilities where poor folks who couldn't afford healthcare would go to get medical attention. As a hobby, Granddaddy's real love was to work on cars; he was a mechanic in his own right. He turned his garage into a car repair shop, and the young men of the neighborhood would flock to him to get help with their clunkers and bask in his talent and advice. Some called him "Mr. Davidson" and others called him "Brother Dave." He was very generous at times by not charging them full price for their repairs. At other times he would teach them all about the secret world of the inside of a car, so they could do their own mechanic work and not have to depend on anyone for small jobs and save their hard earned money.

With Granddaddy's ability to work a full-time job, receive benefits, and have an honest hustle on the side, my grandmother never had to work. I'm sure Granddaddy took pride in that as a man.

I loved my granddaddy more than anything on this earth. I can barely remember, but I have been told that he took me with him all the time. Grandma said he had a bottle warmer that he would plug into his car and away we would go. I vividly remember driving with him in the evenings when he would take me to the foot of the river. We would get us a bag of those hot peanuts from the peanut man who yelled, "Get those hot roasted peanuts here!" Then we would sit on a bench by the dock of the bay, eating our peanuts and watching the boats go by. Mother told me once that my second words ever spoken besides "Da-Da" were "See the boats, see the boats!" As you know, at that age we said everything twice. The best part about our evening river trips was watching the waves that would follow behind the boats, then looking up in the sky at the seagulls flying over the ocean…It was so serene and relaxing. I would fall asleep not knowing when we'd return home and wake up in my bed the next day. Oh what a good night sleep, I would have. A lot of times my granddaddy and I would lie in his bed watching TV; I loved this time with him. He would make the best butter popcorn and kool-aid in the world to me. I remember how sad I was when I was told I couldn't lay in the bed with him anymore because I had developed into a young lady and it wasn't appropriate; I bet my grandma was happy because she got her husband and her bed back to herself.

Grandma was a strong Christian woman and was often the person who encouraged the family to go to church every Sunday, even though my granddaddy would never accompany us.

"Don't believe in giving the preacher all that money," he would say.

"Why are you always cooking something for the Pastor?" Granddaddy would challenge her.

But she never paid his side comments any mind, she was devoted to the church regardless...

Throughout the week Grandma was very busy. Monday night was designated for cleaning the church, Tuesday night choir rehearsal, Wednesday night bible study, Thursday night was senior meetings, and Friday was prayer service. On Saturdays she helped prepare food for the homeless, and the church dinners, and on Sunday morning she took us to Sunday school, before church services. Although my grandma was a devoted member of our church, she never neglected her home or her husband.

I didn't mind going to church as a child at all. There were perks to going to church, mainly because my grandma would always take us out to eat after service. We would gather at my favorite neighborhood restaurant across the street, that some actually referred to as the local "hole in the wall." I would always order my two sloppy joes served on hot dog buns, and for dessert, a double scoop of butter pecan ice cream.

We attended church at Greater Temple Missionary Baptist Church, during my elementary years. As I became older, I went to Burnett Baptist Church and St. James Missionary Baptist Church, where I attended with my mother as a teenager. The late great Rev. Charles Nicks, pastor, a phenomenal preacher and teacher; also known for playing the organ. Some would say, "He made it talk" and was very close friends with Rev. James Cleveland, another musical pioneer who would visit our church often.

I don't ever recall my father going to church. Father was a good looking man, five feet nine inches tall, with olive skin and hazel eyes. He wore a pompadour, one of the most popular hair styles in the early '60s and a do-rag to hold his hair in place. He was known by many as "Eldorado Roy" because he always drove a beautiful candy apple red convertible Cadillac Eldorado with white leather interior. Along with being a street corner crooner he was a hustler in the streets, and I would find out later, he sold plenty of heroin in his day. I've been told that my father was in a gang called the "Dirty Thirties" which he started with his brother and twenty-eight of his closest friends. Eldorado Roy wasn't any ordinary father; he introduced me to drugs at an early age. My belief is that he was trying to use "reverse psychology"; if you let your children try things at home and "school" them, they'll be less likely to sneak and try them later. Needless to say...*It didn't work well with me...*

Being in my father's company was always welcomed, yet an inconsistent treat. When I was able to spend time with him, he would pick me up from my grandparents' house and take me on drives all around Detroit, in areas that were unfamiliar and seemed spooky to me—but at least I was with him and that's all that mattered to me. I loved when he'd take me to some of his stomping grounds. We would go to his favorite restaurant where he was well-known by the owners and patrons alike. He and I would sit at the counter bar, eating and talking for hours. During this time people would come giving him handshakes and high fives, while exchanging money and dope at the same time.

In my father's eyes, I was daddy's girl and he made it

his business to shower me with gifts to prove it. One of my favorite past-times with him was getting my hair done by a lady named Ms. Kelly at a neighboring beauty shop next door to the restaurant. She was this burly heavy set lady with really dark skin. She wore a big house dress, these flat ugly shoes, and a wig that seemed to be on backwards all the time; but boy could she press some hair. I had long, thick course hair that came down to the middle of my back. I would sit for long hours in her chair while she shampooed, conditioned, braided my hair into pig-tails and sat me under a overhead dryer. Then, she'd massage my scalp with grease that looked a lot like lard and skillfully use her utensils to detangle, press and curl my hair. All of that attention would make me feel really pretty and even though Ms. Kelly looked scary, she was like a fairy godmother to me.

Another one of my father's stops was to his joint (house) to "re-up" as it's called, to stock up on more drugs when they were out. He would tell me to sit down on the couch and don't move. Back then parents didn't have to tell their children twice to do something. I knew there were severe consequences, and disobeying my parents was not an option. Sitting there on the couch wallowing in my resentment of having to sit still, I was very observant of my surroundings. From where I was seated, I could see people going into the bathroom to vomit, while the others were tying up their arms, using needles and different things I wasn't aware of. I began to wonder, *"Why are we here?"* but my father never told me and I wasn't allowed to question grown folks business. One time, he caught me staring at one of the junkies and he slammed the door, leaving me frightened and all alone. What was behind the door? Was Daddy doing what I saw the others do? There were many questions I had for my father, but wouldn't dare ask. It was a long time before I realized that my father was not a junkie; he was the drug dealer.

It was important to my father that I was street savvy along with my book sense. He introduced me to drugs at the tender age of eleven. He would sit me down at his favorite restaurant and school me on the different types of drugs he thought I should know about. He would lay pills on the counter, point to them and say, "You don't want to do this one or you don't want to do that one and make sure you don't do this one…" one pill at a time. One time he took a pill, broke a piece off and gave it to me. After we left the restaurant, I was walking down the street with him and saw a puddle of water. Like most children, I leaped to jump over it. I thought I did, but I actually jumped right in it. The pill had me laughing, feeling funny and off balance. Then I told him, laughing, "I kind of like this one dad." He told me, "No, you don't want to like any of them. I just wanted you to see what it would do and how you would react."

After I came down from the effects of it, he explained what it was and why I reacted that way. As a result of the times I spent with my dad, I became familiar with a lot of things I encountered later in high school. When I was offered different pills I would say, "NO I don't want that, don't want that either. NO! I don't want any of that…NO! NO! NO!" You might have thought I would have never used drugs. After all, I knew all about the streets from personal experiences from my own father, and I knew all about drugs the same way. Ironically, I was pretty smart in school in spite of my somewhat unconventional upbringing…*But it didn't add up that way…*

My parents were not the happily ever after story; quite the contrary. I saw my parents argue and fight—a lot. They were young, so I'm sure that hormones helped to flame tempers. I didn't know why they were fighting; I just knew I didn't like it. Whenever it happened, I would be in the other room crying my little heart out, scared to death. My father didn't live with us but would often come over and go into the bedroom with my mom. I noticed sometimes when they came out of the bedroom they would be arguing. One particular day, I heard many things being said and many things being thrown around. The bed post hit up against the wall several times, and lamps were breaking. My mother would come running out of the room, down the stairs, into the kitchen to get a butcher knife. She'd heard that my dad had gotten another woman pregnant. My dad would lock the door to the bedroom and Mom would bang on the door, trying to get in. "Leroy open the door…Open the door, Leroy!" she shouted.

I would run out of my room crying, only to see the butcher knife in her hand, "Mama what are you doing?" I'd ask.

"Nothing baby, get back in the room," she replied.

"No Mama, I want Daddy."

Suddenly my grandparents would return home. My parents were very good at hiding things from them—things like sex, the arguing, and the fighting. By the time my grandparents came in the house, things would have calmed down.

"See you later," my father would say to them.

It was as if nothing had ever happened. Later I found out one of the reasons for all the fighting; in addition to his wandering eyes, Dad had a gambling problem too. Some days he'd come home with lots of money which would excuse him from all the days of not being home or having no money at all; that would start the battles…*This was the village that raised me…*

The most painful memory isn't something I can remember but nonetheless remains fresh in my mind through the stories of others. Trying to remember from pieces of conversation with my mom, bits and fragments over the years have helped me to piece my life together…no…*back* together. After all, it is our stories that have the power to save us. Mom tells me whenever she recounts the story…

"Your granddaddy and I were coming back home from

an errand, when the police contacted me," she explained. "I went immediately to the jail; I knew your dad was dealing. I tried to explain to the police that your dad was a diabetic, not a dope fiend. Because they knew he was dealing heroin, they thought he was going through withdrawal; but he was actually going into a diabetic coma from not having his insulin. Your granddaddy worked at Herman Keifer, which was directly across the street from the police station. He called the hospital for help and they sent an ambulance for your dad and rushed him to the emergency room. The doctors were setting him up with an IV so they could examine him and determine how to treat him. They waited so long to give him his insulin; your dad suffered as a result of the diabetes, and went into a coma and died. Now, I got to come home and tell my little girl her father is dead. Your granddaddy and I sat you down at the table…"

"I have something to tell you, your daddy honey, he died today," said Granddaddy, "but don't worry baby, I'm here."

I'll never forget how tenderly he broke the news to me. Mom ended up suing the city and the Detroit Police Department for "Negligence" on my father's behalf.

JULY 10, 1942 — JANUARY 27, 1971

CHAPTER TWO

During my childhood, I had two main passions, the first one was bowling and my second was skating—it was my true love. When I share with people that I have traveled the world in roller skating competitions, some almost don't believe me. You've probably heard of ice skating competitions more than roller skating, but believe me, they do exist. You have to understand, I was good! Remember that story about me coming home in the middle of the night from skating? I did that every weekend as I became older. My friends and I would skate eight to ten hours at a time, and go from one skating rink to another, as long as they were open. One day, a white male came to the Arena Skating Rink, one of Detroit's most popular skating rinks. He was watching several skaters, and of course, one of them was me. I guess you could say I was "discovered"—that is, me and my friends.

It was 1968, one year after the infamous Detroit urban rebellion, the riots of 1967 that were part of a frustrated fever that hit cities around the country; a rebellion born out of a cauldron of injustice, inequities and sanctioned violence to black minds and bodies. White Detroiters started moving out and the majority of the city would soon become black, but for the time being, our skating rinks and our factory jobs were still thriving.

The white male was a skating coach and a pretty intelligent guy. He knew that the cities were a treasure filled with competitive athletic talent. At this particular skating rink, the custom was to stagger orange cones around the perimeter of the rink. We would line up at the starting line, the whistle would blow and the skaters would take off racing. The cones helped to keep us on the right path. After two laps, we would come across the finish line as first, second, and third place winners. We'd then receive a gift certificate as a prize to buy things from the concession stand or from the hobby shop inside the rink...*I wish I'd paid attention to the "cones" in my life...*

This man who would become my skating coach approached the floor guard who was supervising the skaters from the race, and asked, "Who would you say are the best skaters here?" The floor guard pointed to several people, among them was Cookie, Marlon, Debbie, Byron, Steve, Stevie, Ava, and I. Coach Burt, as he was called, moved quickly to put together a team, and off we went every weekend to Ambassador Roller Rink in Clawson, Michigan for our training. Our first competition was in Rochester, Michigan. Our team didn't win, at least not the team competitions anyway. As a team we came in fifth place. The other teams were much better; they were virtually all-white skating teams who were used to this level of competition. Yet, we were inspired and encouraged to continue on. We left the rink that day saying **"We can do this!"**

In 1971, our team came into its own. We went back to Rochester, Michigan to compete in the four-women relays, and won, beating six other teams. We were the first African-American four-women relay team to ever win. From Rochester, Michigan we went on to Akron, Ohio and won again! From there it was on to the semi-finals in "chi-town"— Chicago, Illinois. We were traveling by car, and by this time my mother was the designated driver. My mother convinced Grandmother to come along and experience the races first hand, because we would stay up late telling her every detail. Grandmother was a woman who believed in saving money big time; she would cook all the fixings to travel with: fried chicken in a shoebox that would be layered with paper towels on the bottom of the box to catch all the grease and seasonings, a big bowl of potato salad, a loaf of bread, chips, home-made pound cake and canned sodas. "Don't eat it all," my mother admonished me, "You know you shouldn't eat too much before your skate meet."

My mother was my best cheerleader; I think she en-joyed it as much as I did. The traveling, the competing, the roaring of the crowds and making sure my pig-tails were in place. In Chicago, we won again! Next would be the semi-finals and then on to compete in the Nationals at the Will Rogers Coliseum in Dallas, Texas.

We had a little setback in Dallas, but it had nothing to do with skating. Mom, Grandma, my teammate Debbie and I went to breakfast that morning. It was the crack of dawn, about four-thirty or five o'clock and the waitress kept passing us by, waiting on the other tables that were seated after us. Time was passing fast and by the time she walked past us again, my mother snatched the waitress by the collar.

"Are you going to wait on us or not?" she said force-fully. "I should whip your ass." She was mad enough to spit bricks.

"They're going to put you in jail," my grandma warned my mother.

"I don't care," my mother retorted. Then she contin-ued. "You walked back and forth, back and forth, and you never asked us one time if we wanted something to eat."

But it was 1972, a few years after the Greensboro sit-ins that broke the dam and beat the death knoll of rude, dehu-manizing lunch counter segregation in the South... but still no food. By this time, my grandma had gotten mad.

"This is utterly ridiculous; we have two children and you walk past again and didn't say anything! Where's the owner?"

The owner of the establishment came out and apologized, offering to feed us. "Never mind, I don't want anything," my mother told him. We never got anything to eat, and by the time they finished ignoring us it was too close to race time and we ran the risk of cramping.

Although my mother wasn't a professional skating coach, she was never short of advice. "Listen! Get in front first and lead the pack. If you get in front first, they'll have to catch you," she would tell me...*Ever notice how good sports lessons are also good life lessons...*

We arrived at the very large Will Rogers Coliseum. Talk about skaters! There were skaters from all over the world in this place—Professional skaters that were world champions with ten or more years of experience. Desperately, I wanted to win in our category. I had more determination than I had talent that morning. But I had to trust and believe in myself that I, Tanya, could do this. I couldn't think of anything more gratifying than to **WIN** this race!

They were calling for us to come and check-in; we were completely dressed in our uniforms. Our colors were black and gold. We had on black tights, a black shirt with a gold strip that ran around the front and the back, and black shorts with two thin gold strips down the side. We had black skate covers to cover our skates, and gold wrist bands to match. We looked really hot with our team name, Clawson, Michigan and our number written on our backs. I surmised that the other skaters had never had to race black skaters before. I couldn't be positive, but I was sure they thought black skaters weren't experienced enough. These other teams started competing when they were babies.

Cookie was the anchor of our team and no one could catch her. She, Steve and Bryon came in first in every category they entered. In our category Debbie and I would share first and second.

It was time. We were up next; I remember I could see Grandma in her seat praying as usual and my mother gearing up to watch the race. We had Debbie as the starter, I was second, Ava third and Cookie as our anchor; the line-up was perfect.

Debbie was at the starting line, waiting on the whistle to blow. It blew and Debbie took off and around the first corner; she was out in front. Debbie was very tall with long legs, and if she got in front, it was hard to catch her.

I was next. My heart was beating; it felt like it was going to pop out of my chest. While standing there I said to myself, *"You can do this, you can do this. All I need to do is keep the pace, don't fall behind and I've done my part."* I had the baton. *"Stay focused Tanya,"* I said. Yet, all I could hear was the crowd cheering. The girl behind me was gaining on my tail. I couldn't let her pass me; I had one more lap to go. My legs were getting tired but I couldn't give up, I was too close to the end. All I had to do was give the baton to Ava and I had done my part for the team…my hand was out to pass the baton to Ava. She had it! We were still in first place! "Go Ava! Go! Go!" I was yelling at the top of my lungs.

Ava was small and petite and I swear she could go between your legs if you had them wide enough; she was so fast. She was coming around the third cone into the third lap with one more lap to go. Still yelling, "Go! Go!" Then all of a sudden…Ava went down. Second place was now in front, third and fourth place was a half lap behind. Even though Ava went down, she got up quickly, keeping us in second place about a quarter mile behind before passing the baton to Cookie.

Cookie was one of the fastest skaters I've ever known so I knew we still had a chance. She was gaining up on first place with one lap to go. "Go Cookie! Go!" I kept screaming. I closed my eyes. I couldn't look; I would cover my eyes then peek to glance through, then I'd turn quickly because I didn't want to see what was about to happen. I looked over at my mother; she and the whole crowd were up on their feet and my grandma's head was down, of course, praying. Cookie had caught up with first place. Oh my God... Cookie's toe stop had come off her skate around the last turn; I thought it was her wheel. "Go! Cookie, Go! Go! Go!" We all yelled." History was in the making; the first black four-women relay team to win nationals.

The race was over; **WE WON!** Even the press wrote a story about us. I can't tell you how proud I was of myself and our team. Looking over at Mom and Grandma, I could see they were just as happy as I was as we were standing for pictures with our huge trophy and a beautiful wood-plaque. All the hard work that year paid off, and to see all the people congratulating us was an awesome feeling, especially from other ethnic people. I think from that experience, my mother and Grandma's opinion about other races had changed. It was that day, we felt like equals.

CHAPTER THREE

Herman Gardens, a predominantly white housing development on Detroit's northwest side—where my cousins lived. They were the only black family that lived there at that time. Herman Gardens was a public housing project built during the 1930s in an era that was named by historians as the "golden age" of public housing. Detroit's reputation even as one of the most segregated cities in the country had its roots in that era. With public housing strictly segregated by race, the Brewster's were "black", Herman Gardens, "white".

I thought my cousins were very wealthy at the time, because the housing they lived in was really nice and new—not like the neighborhood I lived in. After the black families started moving in, the housing development became what is now known as "The Projects." I would visit my cousins frequently on the weekends, and became very familiar with the people and the families in that community.

When it came time for me to attend high school, my mom insisted I attend Frank Cody High School, a multi-cultural school closer to my cousin's address than my own. My mother didn't want me to attend Northwestern High School in our area, because it had a bad reputation since the '60s. So, I commuted back and forth to school in a brand new 1975 Ford Elite that my mother purchased for me. It was white with burgundy interior, fully loaded, and paid for in full with the money that was awarded to me from my father's death. I would pick up my friends: Kim, Michelle (whom we called "Mickey"), and my cousin Wanda every day at the bus stop along the way. It was as if I was the bus driver stopping at the bus stop every morning like clock-work.

We were the four "musketeers", and we did everything together. We had our own unique style and we wore it well. We would wear these three-piece suits with vests that were fitted to our bodies with a shirt and tie. When we went out to the night clubs we would throw on Borsalino hats and boutonnieres to match. These outfits were very sexy, especially with our two and a half inch pumps. Sometimes we would even throw on a pimp chain to really set things off. Kim was my closest friend, just like Barbara and I were when I was younger; when you saw me, you saw Kim and vice versa.

In 1975 at Cody High there were a small percentage of blacks in attendance. I'd say about thirty percent black and seventy percent white. On Fridays, some students would still get into racial fights with each other and we would be outnumbered and have to run to the McDonalds for safety, where I would sometime park my car.

In class I was a pretty good student and had to keep my grades up to par, because as long as I did, I was able to go skating in the evenings. I wasn't a girl who skipped school to hang out with friends or anything like that, but there were a few times that I did miss school to get some rest due to skating all night. Yet, I still had to be responsible for making sure my school work was done and turned in on time. Skating would be the first thing Mom would take away from me as a punishment. But I'd rather take the "Whooping" that Granddaddy would give me than not be able to go skating, and my parents knew that.

My friends and I were considered the "stuck-up" girls. We hung out with other girls who were considered snobbish, and stuck up too. One of our schoolmate's families would have great functions at their home on the weekends. Her home was a three-story colonial with five bedrooms, and a finished basement. Not like ours on Pacific Street, but more like something you would see in Architectural Digest. They had an in-ground pool, with a wrap-around patio with all the furnishings in a yard that looked like an oasis and boy could her family throw a party. So between my family, friends, surroundings, life travels and the exposure I had to some of the world, I experienced a life of *Possibilities...*

My life was not a bad life at all. Unfortunately, I had a curious side. I was the type of girl who liked to experiment and test the waters. I would call myself a go-getter. Now those characteristics may not be considered that bad, but you have to be careful how they are directed and in what way you use them. Mom would often tell me, "You're just like your dad." She saw that hustler in me that he had in him...*But there was an underlying tone here...*

My first boyfriend was Michael Brown who was known as Man Brown, a real cutie. When we dated, we did what we called "Dutch" dating. Remember Dutch dating?— when the guy and the girl paid their own way on a date. We loved to meet at the skating rink or at the theater. Back then for a guy just to put his arm around you or sneak a kiss before leaving was a really big thing. When we'd return to our homes, we would talk on the phone all night until our parents or grandparents said "Get off the phone and go to sleep"— such an innocent and nice time for me it was "Puppy Love".

Then there was Tony Johnson. Tony was fine as wine, a senior in high school with his own car. He drove a green Monte Carlo with a white vinyl top and white leather interior. He lived on the Northwest side of Detroit, which was considered the upper middle-class area. Most of the people who lived in that neighborhood were very educated: attorneys, teachers, engineers, and actually some of the employers of the big three—Ford, Chrysler, and GM.

Tony was my first real love and the one whom I lost my virginity to. He was the first to expand my horizons by wining and dining me. He took me out constantly to different restaurants, concerts and stage plays. He was romantic and very popular in high school.

Tony's family was into numbers racketeering and made plenty of money. They were probably one of the top three largest racketeering families in the state of Michigan. Being around them was an introduction to some of the finer things in life, which excited me. They had a beautiful home, the nicest cars; a ranch filled with horses, a yacht and wore some of the finest clothing. His mother was a confident and gorgeous business woman, whom I admired. I loved how she ran her household, took good care of her husband and able to afford a maid and a cook, all while running a business.

Tony was employed by his family, picking up numbers in the morning and in the evenings along with other employees, earning approximately five-hundred dollars a week while still in high school. When I became closer to the family, they also employed me with a job making four-hundred dollars a week. My job consisted of going through all the tickets, and checking the numbers for hits to pay out to the winners, and then add up all the tickets' profit. Between the two of us, and all the perks and bonuses that came along with the job, we made a whole lot of money at a very young age.

Tony had an entrepreneur spirit, which was something I became to love about him. He started promoting some of the best parties in Detroit's downtown area in a club named Studio 54—one of the hottest spots in town. He themed his parties uniquely taken from groups like Devo, the B52's, and Blondie. Once the parties started, I was the girl in the booth who collected all the money. I thought my position was one of importance, and of course I was Tony Johnson's girl.

The year was 1977, and on this particular day I decided to make a trip down stairs, underground where the party was going on. This was something I had never done before; I usually just handled the money and would be escorted home. I saw Tony and some of our friend's smoking weed, snorting cocaine and pissy drunk. I was stunned but said nothing about my concern; I just kept dancing and socializing, acting like I hadn't seen anything at all. The first chance I got alone with Tony I confronted him, "When did you all start doing drugs like that?"

I knew he smoked a joint or two but never cocaine. People would always say his parties were a blast, and now I knew why. Even some of TV's celebrities that came into town would end up at his parties. One in particular I remember was Darnell Williams, who played the role of Jessie Hubbard on "All my Children". I was shocked, for I had admired the soap opera actor for years, following him and Debbie Morgan, who played the role of Angie. It bothered me, but I didn't say any-thing…It wasn't me, it wasn't my life, and besides I had been schooled by "Eldorado Roy", my daddy.

Chapter Four

In 1979, my best friend Kim moved to California. She wanted me to move out there with her but I was still in a relationship with Tony at that time and I didn't want to leave him. Later that year, Tony and I departed as friends; the night life consumed him—the women and the drugs that is.

Kim would write me letters telling me all about how well she was doing. She was dating a Hollywood doctor, living in a really nice home right off Venice beach and driving a Rolls Royce. I had to get out there to see what was going on because it was not just California but Hollywood, California. Back in the day, going to Los Angeles, Las Vegas, or New York was like going to Paris or Rome. People would have to save for months or even years to go to these places. After hearing about the wonderful things Kim was involved in, I decided to visit and see for myself. I went with the intentions of never returning, hoping for that big break like Darnell and Debbie.

Everybody knew I was going to L.A.; I'd been telling people about the many dreams I had of being in a soap opera or becoming a movie actress. This was my one and only chance and I was going to take full advantage of it.

While preparing for my big trip, my neighbors and family were helping me prepare too. They loaded me up with all types of things—not just the chicken in a shoebox, but sandwiches, pop, and snacks for my trip. It was kind of embarrassing because I was going on an airplane, not on a road trip, but refusing would have been disrespectful. In our era this had always been a longtime tradition when someone was nesting away. So there I was getting on an airplane chicken in a shoebox and a carry-on bag full of food theless, I was thrilled.

Flying into LAX Airport, looking out the window, and seeing that "Hollywood" sign all lit up, was pure excitement. The moment I got off the plane I was screaming, "I'm here LA, I'm here!" Kim was there to pick me up and seeing her again brought back such great memories. I was anticipating everything she talked about in her letters. First, it was hugs and kisses. It had been a while since I last saw her, and she looked amazing. Kim had a figure that excited most men. She had a small waist, nice hips, gorgeous legs and her hair was still long, thick and blue-black. She was light skinned and in the '70s, light skinned girls were priceless. I was a brown skinned girl with long beautiful black hair, huge breasts and skinny legs and together, we never had a problem with the men. We were the Salt-n-Pepa of our day.

While walking to get my luggage she was telling me all about the party we were going to attend. I was so excited. I asked her, "Am I dressed okay or should I change into something else?"

She replied, "Girl, you're fine." However, I was taken off guard when she asked me, "Have you ever "freebased" before?"

To be honest, I didn't know what in the world she was talking about. I wanted her to think I knew, but I didn't. I wanted to fit in so I replied, "Yeah, I do."

My desire to fit in became an opportunity the enemy used to lure me down a path of heartbreak and near destruction...

"We're going to a freebase party," said Kim brightly. "It's at the house of a celebrity's daughter."

When she told me who the celebrity's daughter was; that made me even more excited. I was going to be around the people I needed to meet in order to carry out my dreams and make my plan work. As a matter of fact, we put the bags right in the trunk and went straight to the party. When we arrived, there were celebrities everywhere. The few that I feel comfortable mentioning are the ones who later came forth publicly about their drug problems—Natalie Cole, and Richard Pryor.

The evening festivities didn't start out like any party I had ever been to in the past. This party was different. For instance, throughout the house there were board games, but not your average size board games. These were life size board game sets on painted floors replicating whatever game you were playing; like backgammon and chess. Just to see this type of chess game left me astonished and I immediately signed up to play. You literally had to pick up the pieces and carry them to make your next move. It was like carrying a light-weight statue and it was phenomenal. The backgammon board also took up a whole floor. Where I came from we had a set that came with checkers, chess and backgammon pieces inside with a double sided board that accommodated all of them in one.

While watching all the people networking, dancing, and socializing; looking like money, money, money. Kim walks in the room and whispered to me, "Come here, I want to show you something." We entered into another room filled with people doing all sorts of drugs. As we sat down on this beautiful Italian couch, someone placed a plate of white powder, right in front of me on a clear acrylic cocktail table. I thought it was cocaine. I had seen this before at one of Tony's parties. I had watched them take a card and scoop the cocaine on the corner of it and then sniff the powder up one of their nostrils… I remembered that. So I was getting ready to pick up a card to sniff some up my nostril when they yelled, "Noooo!"

Startled, I said to Kim, "What?" That's when she told

me it was freebase and it goes in the pipe. Kim began to tell me what to do and how to do it. She put the freebase in the pipe and said, "When I light it, you pull the smoke in, hold your nose for about three seconds, then blow it out." After I did what she said, she asked how I felt. I told her, "I didn't feel anything."

I really wasn't interested in the freebasing, but I did it a couple more times before we left the room just to be sociable—I didn't think it would hurt... *Here I was doing something again to fit in.*

We walked into another room where people were playing a game, not the ordinary games I knew about, but with "Freebase" called the "World Series." In this particular room there was a dining room table that sat twenty people. The four people in the middle that sat across from each other would smoke from a pipe that had four stems on it. As soon as those four got up from the table, four more people rotated down to the middle, and the World Series started all over again.

"If you don't pull hard you probably won't get any," they told me.

There I sat with the pros. I tried several times, pulling as hard as I could, and got nothing, felt nothing. "Freebase" was a substance which is now referred to as "Crack." But freebase was cocaine that was mixed with "Ether" and water in a small vial. The Ether would separate the chemicals apart from the cocaine to bring it to its purest form. You would then take a dropper and remove everything from the separation line in the vial and absorb it into the dropper. Then squeeze the substance out on a plate or glass surface to dry, turning it back into a powder form. That's why I assumed it was just cocaine...*This was different, and a little more serious substance.*

When we returned to her home that night, the only thing I noticed from the encounter I had with the freebasing was insomnia. I really didn't like the feeling of not being able to sleep. That's when Kim handed me a pill, and I asked, "What's this?" "A *Valium* to help you sleep," she said. Even though it looked like one of the pills my father had showed me, I took it with a glass of milk anyway. It was in a prescription bottle, so it seemed legal and safe to take.

The next morning I was having trouble waking up. Kim wanted to take me sightseeing and shopping. "I'm so tired...I'm still so sleepy," I complained. "Here, take one of these." Kim gave me a *Quaalude,* which was an "upper", to wake me up. I washed it down with a glass of orange juice, and thought, "Well her friend is a doctor and they're prescription drugs; how bad could they be?"

At this point, I hadn't been in Los Angeles twenty-four hours and had consumed three different types of drugs that I had never taken before in my entire life. It was only by the grace of *God* that my body suffered no ill side effects...*At lease none that I knew about at the time.*

Kim and I went shopping and she showed me around L.A. It was different, exciting, and delightful and I was thrilled about the warm weather; NO SNOW either. Los Angeles had the beaches, the piers, luxury cars and the shopping on Rodeo Drive. I felt like a kid in a candy store.

As we strolled into a beautiful boutique, I discovered a pair of boots that jumped out at me. These boots weren't any ordinary pair of boots you would see just anywhere; they were a light shade of emerald green I'd never seen before. A cow-girl-like boot with a three and a half inch heel, and down the side they were adorned with precious jewelry of all sorts: rhinestones, gold and silver studs and strands of pearls. We continued through the store searching for an outfit to match and found an all-white suit with an embroidery design on the back; that looked fabulous on me. I don't think I would have ever purchased this type of outfit in Detroit, but in L.A., I was feeling like I was one of the stars.

The jewelry Kim purchased for me was one of a kind and coordinated very well. Of course, we didn't put this ensemble together ourselves; a fashion stylist who worked at the boutique had been catering to our every need. My measly savings of one thousand dollars was dwindling quickly; as you could probably imagine in L.A. everything was expensive—especially, when you shop till you drop.

Later that night, while we were preparing to go experience California's night life, Kim's boyfriend returned home from work. I had already known all about him from all our letters back and forth.

"This is my boyfriend Gregory. Gregory, meet my best friend Tanya. Greg's a doctor," she added proudly.

Dr. Gregory Schaefer was dressed to the nines, decked out in a dark blue suit with a baby blue shirt and a multi-colored shaded blue tie. He had dark smooth skin and a full beard that was groomed perfectly. Dr. Schaefer took us and a couple of Kim's other friends out on the town in his Royal Blue Rolls Royce. He really knew how to party in style and he paid for everything. The five course meal included: appetizers, soups, salads and main course to deserts to open bar…sky was the limit.

I was enjoying all the glitz and glamour and the clubs were rocking too. I'm out on the dance floor showing L.A. all my moves, and embracing the wild nightlife. When I glanced over at Kim and her friends, they were snorting cocaine out of this tiny little bottle that had a small spoon attached to it, and popping pills. Kim turned and said to me, "Take this, it's going to keep you up." It was another Quaalude. We partied, taking Quaaludes, snorting cocaine and drinking all night long.

When we returned home that night, the party continued. A crowd of friends followed us back to Kim's house and everyone continued snorting cocaine, drinking, smoking marijuana, playing bid whist, and dancing. But I was exhausted and looking for a bed. I was experiencing jetlag from the three hour time difference, and I began to feel like the party-pooper, the outcast. I was feeling anxious and afraid that I would be called out for not being a part of their lifestyle.

The next morning, I was feeling terrible. I called to talk to my mother, "Hey baby! How's it going, are you having a good time," she said.

"I'm coming home mom," I replied.

She quickly responded, "What do you mean you're coming home?"

I replied, "I want to come home early."

Concerned, she asked, "What's wrong?"

I told her, "I'll tell you when I get home."

I went home that morning on the next flight leaving L.A... My trip was cut short. I expected to go to Los Angeles for a two week vacation, in hopes of never returning; turns out my dreams, hopes, and goals flew right by me like the birds flying south for the winter. Los Angeles, California was ten times faster than "The Motor City"—Detroit, that is.

When I returned home I told my mom all about what I had experienced. She assured me that I had done the right thing by leaving an environment that wasn't good to be in.

"I don't think Kim's boyfriend is a doctor," I confided in Mom. "I saw him doing things I didn't think a doctor would do around us and all the different types of drugs I began to use, I just wasn't comfortable."

Later, Kim confided in me that he wasn't actually a doctor. He was able to obtain fake credentials in order to push illegal drugs. In those days in Los Angeles, you could buy yourself just about any college degree to be whoever you wanted to be. As it turned out, he was also into pharmaceuticals, creating his own white and pink cocaine. He would give out those drugs to anyone that was paying and write prescriptions for any kind of drug that people were willing to buy. From what I experienced, I didn't care to partake in their lifestyle of being a part of the rich and famous. Kim had painted a beautiful picture of how her life was great and from the outside looking in, it was. But inside, she was actually tearing herself down …

The next day I met up with my friends; they were shocked and concerned about me being back so soon. I explained the things I had experienced to them.

"See, we mixed the cocaine in water and then we smoked it through a glass pipe," I told them.

"That's a weed pipe," they would retort. "You've got it all mixed up. You must have been trippin; all those pills probably got you confused."

They were making me feel like I didn't know what I was talking about. No one believed me, but I knew what I had seen and done on my trip and I wasn't going to back down from my stories.

After I had been home a while, one of my friends called me saying, "There's a guy from Los Angeles here and he has that glass pipe with the freebase you were telling us about."

"See girl, I told you that's what I had!" I told her.

"He's coming over to my house tonight around seven…Come on by, I want to introduce him to you, or maybe you already met him while you were out there."

When I arrived at my friend's house, the guy from L.A. was showing everyone how to freebase. His name was

Dwight; he was tall and handsome, with grey eyes and golden brown skin. He was dressed in an all-white suit, yellow shirt and his skin against that color went very well. He had on these nice brown loafers with no socks, and boy was that a turn on! As I continued to look down at the bottom of his pants leg as he sat, you could see his hairy legs with a gold ankle chain to accommodate the look—very sexy. He seemed intelligent and nice. You could tell he was one of L.A.'s finest, but he was here to turn Detroit out and we were his first victims.

I smoked with them. However, *I still* didn't feel like I was being affected by it. *I still* didn't feel like it was addictive. *I still* didn't feel like anything was wrong. I thought it was just something I would do, and then let it go. You know—something sociable like having a glass of wine now and then.

There is a point in everyone's life that there is no return, a point where, if you go beyond it, it is not easy to return back...

CHAPTER FIVE

One day after work, I saw Dwight parked outside of my job. I was a travel agent at Avante` Travel; a travel agency located inside the First National Bank Building downtown, Detroit.

"Hey Dwight," I called to him. "You remember me?"

"Yeah, Tanya right," he replied.

"Yes, how have you been doing," I asked.

"I've been fine," he replied.

"Yes you are," I thought. As I looked into those grey eyes that wandered exactly where most men eyes wandered, right to my breasts. It was something about the people from L.A... They all seemed to look good to me, with that golden brown tan look. We talked for a little, and then the big question came.

"So have you been freebasing lately?" he asked.

"No, not since the last time I saw you," I replied.

"You know, I'm actually on my way to a friend's house to cop and smoke…Are you doing anything later?" he asked.

I had nothing planned, and I was about to get off work. I told him, "I can meet you in twenty minutes."

"Great, meet me at this address," he said.

When I got off work, I drove to the address he had given me. It wasn't on the west side where I lived, and I was unfamiliar with the east side of Detroit; I hadn't traveled over there often. It was always known as the "Gangsta" side of town. Most of Detroit's after hour joints were located on the east side and prostitution and pimps were known commonly on that side too.

As I pulled up in front of the address he had given me; he was still in the car, and I was glad. I parked behind him and waited until he got out of his car, so we could walk up to the house together—the house reminded me of one of the houses my father would go to. His friend Dray came to the door. He introduced us as we entered the house. Dray was not as attractive as Dwight, but he wasn't a bad looking guy. He just seemed a bit street, a little hood-ish.

The house was old and worn down. With old furnishings, ancient wood floors, dust and spider webs and a smell I couldn't describe. He escorted us straight to a room in the attic. There laid a mattress on the floor, a milk crate as a night stand a glass pipe on top, a lighter and an ashtray full of butts. I had asked myself the same question years before when I was with my father, *"Why are we here?"*

This wasn't the ordinary atmosphere I was used to. Where were the people that looked like Dwight? Where were the doctors, and the celebrities?

He pulled out the freebase cocaine, put some in the pipe and handed it to me to go first. I hesitated for a moment, nervous, in this unfamiliar place. I was feeling a little bit like I did that night in L.A... But it didn't stop me from taking the pipe out of his hand or the broken hanger with a cotton ball on the end that was dipped in alcohol, and use it as a torch once it was lit.

Lighting the freebase inside the stem and pulling like my friend Kim had shown me, you would have thought I was a pro at it. Yet I was unaware of the true scope of my trouble. The only thing I knew right then was the rapture of the smoke entering into my lungs, as I remembered to hold it for three seconds as they all instructed me to do. With my head towards the ceiling and my eyes closed, I then blew out every bit of smoke that was inside my mouth; this time the feeling was different. Could it have been because I had nothing around me to distract me from this high like I had before? There was no one here that I had to try to fit in with; it was just me and the guys. Somehow, I started to feel free and comfortable with no pressure to conform to. I felt different and I wanted another…

I call heaven and Earth to record this day against you, that I have set before you life and death, blessings and curses, therefore, choose life that both you and your descendants will live…

Deuteronomy 30:13

I wish, at that pivotal moment, I had chosen life…

Dwight was preparing to leave for Los Angeles and maybe I had had too much, but still wanting more, he suggested I stay with Dray, "You'll be alright staying here with Dray, Dray's my man, he won't let anything happen to you… Trust me."

After Dwight left, Dray and I continued to get high. Dray was the "middle man", the go between guy that took all the risks; and we were running out of money. Dray told me if I wanted to, I could pawn my ring at a pawnshop in exchange for money. He promised to get it back the next day after he got paid from some job. The next thing I knew, all my jewelry was pawned: my necklace, bracelet, earrings, watch and ring. The next day Dray did receive money from his job but we did not return to the pawnshop to pick up my jewelry—His money went up in smoke too.

After getting high for two days straight and with no money left to get high with, I was ready to go home. I didn't want to return home without my jewelry, because I knew my grandparents or my mom would notice. And what was I going to say about being gone for two days and not calling anyone? Sitting there in agony, I came up with...

"Hit me in the eye," I told Dray.

"Girl you want me to do what? You must be crazy as hell," he said.

"You have to because I can't go home without my jewelry, I need an excuse," I replied.

Dray obliged, and I found myself at the police station telling this big lie! My granddaddy was the one who came to pick me up, looking at me with the saddest eyes.

"What happened to you?" he asked, with his eyes boring into me. He knew there was more to my story. I had never lied to him before, and I didn't have the courage to tell him the truth. I was closer to him than my own mother and he knew me so well... He saw a look about me that let him know it was more to my story than me just being attacked. Lying to my granddaddy was more painful than getting hit in the eye.

When we returned to the house, my family nurtured me, fed me and tried to love me back to my normal life. But, Granddaddy wore a look of disappointment on his face and it kept playing over and over in my head. I heard him and my grandmother talking in the other room, my granddaddy crying; he couldn't understand what had gone wrong. Of course, Grandmother was reassuring him, "All we can do is pray. The Lord will take care of her; we have to put this in *God's* hands," she said to him.

Three days later, I was back at Dray's house; I wanted to get high bad. I wanted to forget about the disappointment and the lie I had told to my granddaddy. Thinking, *"If I could just see the cloud inside the pipe, I would escape from all the pain I had just caused."* I didn't know anyone else but Dray to go to because Dwight was back in L.A. I had no clue of how to get the paraphernalia nor did I know where to cop. I had to rely on Dray to get high and...this would become a vicious cycle.

I was not only giving up my jewelry, but my body as well...

"Jeffery will take care of you, but only if you have sex with him," Dray said to me.

At first, I couldn't wrap my mind around what I was about to do. I was the person who always said I'd never prostitute my body. Prostitution for me was a NO, NO, but the drug dealer was dressed to impress and he smelled real good when he walked towards me. The cologne was enticing, he was well groomed, and it made my task easier. But I had only one thing on my mind—getting high, frankly at that point anyone would have probably looked good.

This vicious cycle continued. I would be gone for days and my family would be worried out of their minds. When I'd return home, they would be so angry at me because by this time they knew I was getting high. I would feel bad about what I was putting them through. I would be forced to face the consequences of my actions, and the embarrassment I felt—would only make me want to get high again. When I returned home this time, my mother and grandparents wanted a sit down with me.

"Why are you doing this to yourself?" they would ask me between binges. "We didn't raise you this way. What can we do to help you Tanya?" My grandmother implored.

I knew I was betraying and disappointing them and I felt like I owed it to them to at least try and stay clean. But there was no doubt I was in trouble physically, mentally and spiritually. The problem was trying to figure out what exactly was causing my misery and despair; them or me. What was the nature of my weakness? Then I wrote a letter...

Granddaddy,

I really didn't mean to disappoint you. I love you, Grandmother and my mother so much. I don't know how I got to this point. You raised me better than this. You taught me right from wrong and my mother has supported me in whatever I was doing. My father told me over and over to stay away from this. I hate that this has happened and I hope you can find it in your heart to forgive me. I will try and do better.

Love, Tanya

I decided to at least try to get my life back in order. For a six week respite, I gave myself an opportunity to not get into any trouble. I avoided everyone with whom I had done drugs. Things seemed back to normal. But I didn't do a lot of celebrating and neither did my family. I'm sure they were scared that I would leave again any minute...That's what drug addiction is like. You make promises to yourself and others, you feel determined to stop, and then the desire and the urge simply overtakes you, and your frustration feeds your desperation and you spiral downward and out of control.

"Freebase / Crack" is a mental addiction, more than a physical one. Your mind convinces you that you want it. An addicted person eventually begins to chase a high that they'll never ever reach again. If I learned anything during those six weeks, it was that I had not actually kicked the addiction. I just put it on the back burner. I still wanted the drug itself, even though the desire faded...just a bit. But it wasn't enough... No freebase tonight, I promised myself...

And I know that nothing good lives in me, that is, in my sinful nature, I want to do what is right but I can't. I want to do what is good, but I don't. I don't want to do what is wrong, but I do it anyway...

Romans 7:18

CHAPTER SIX

R ay Lewis…Ray was Tony's so called "Uncle". He and Tony's mother were partners. Ray was the real brains behind the family business and he had always treated me like I was part of the family.

"Tanya!" Ray smiled his biggest smile and gave me a big bear hug. "It's so good to see you."

We talked for a while, and then he invited me to have dinner with him one day. Ever the innocent I agreed, thinking it was a kindly older gentleman treating his pretend "niece" to supper.

"How is Tony's mom? I asked him.

"She's doing fine," he replied.

"How is Tony?"

"Well you know, Tony is Tony," we laughed.

We continued with the small talk about old times. We had such a great time, we set another dinner date. There was a second dinner date, then a third. I began to accompany Ray on several occasions. Soon I started sleeping with him, and after that he began to spoil me with gifts. He purchased me a Cimarron Cadillac and I received a key to one of his places right off the Detroit River—I had a gorgeous view. I frequently met him at a popular gentleman's club on Detroit's East Side, where several of his friends who were black car dealer owners often hung out. There were boat rides and late night soirees, and without anything said, I became Ray's woman. During the course of our dating and besides all the lavish gifts and traveling we did, we became really close; he was someone I could talk to about anything.

I mentioned to Ray about the drugs I had used. I also shared some of the sexual things I had done for the drugs. His curiosity was piqued. The next thing I knew Ray started having cocaine around. I'm not sure if he was doing cocaine before, but I know he wasn't freebasing. Now I was faced with the temptation of getting high again. It wasn't really in my heart to stop doing drugs to begin with; it was for my mother and my grandparents.

Because of Ray's desire to experience those sexual things I had described to him, that caused him to purchase more and more drugs. I'd shown him everything I knew; he even found out where to get the paraphernalia. He opened Pandora's Box and inadvertently got caught up in all of it himself, and now we were both *freebasing*.

The thing that made matters worse; Ray was a married man. I was committing adultery against *God* and he was committing adultery against *God* and his wife. When you are not in your right state of mind, you compromise so much, so much of yourself to feed that addiction. Want to hear something sick? I believed in his own way, Ray loved me. Yet I always knew I should not have been with him...he belonged to someone else.

He constantly promised to divorce his wife, and I really believed him. Yet, for years this lie remained and I continued to be his mistress. Ray's life suffered and the business only persevered because of his partner. Eventually Ray returned back to his wife; he always said, "It is cheaper to keep her." I was the one left alone and I went right back to the streets looking for love in all the wrong places...

...I went looking for Dray; he would always have

drugs in his possession and if he didn't he'd know where to find some. There we were—Dray and I getting high again!

This time, there was a new era and freebasing was now known as "Crack." It reminded me of the fast food era—everything quick, fast, and in a hurry. We no longer had to wait for the mixing and drying process. Crack was the drug that now swept the nation. And it had everybody's name on it; it went looking for any and everyone from the "White House" to the most ghetto neighborhood. It touched all races, creeds, and colors.

But here's the difference; "Crack" has other substances added to it, from "speed" to "comeback" and other hallucinogenic. You would take cocaine, mix with baking soda and add some of these substances I just describe inside a glass heat tempered item and it would form into a solid rock.

> CRACK: One of the most deadly drugs going around the country destroying the human race...

> CRACK: The most intensified high you'll ever experience in your life time: habit forming, addictive, causing the mind to make perpetrating decisions...

> CRACK: Millions and Millions of dollars spent on a small portion, micro-dot size that lasts about sixty-seconds rushing straight to the brain and traveling through the body's blood stream...

> CRACK: You'll lose your respect, your dignity, and your self-esteem. "It happened to me..."

> —*Tanya Davis*

CHAPTER SEVEN

O
n clear nights I'd search for crack like I was looking for the stars in the sky. By now Dray had introduced me to many people and had shown me several different joints to cop from. The price of crack was way cheaper than freebase. These micro–dot size pieces of crack came in small quantity pricing. There were dime joints ($10.00) and nickel joints ($5.00) and sometimes they would have specials like K-Mart's blue light special with $3.00 crack sold for an hour at a time throughout the day.

You could say by now I was "tore up from the floor up". I ate, drank, and slept crack. I would do anything for crack; you name it I did it. I started writing bad checks, committing credit card fraud, stealing and because of the frequent sex, I had many abortions. I did many things that I would later be ashamed of and eventually pay for …

Then, there was Jessie. He was a notorious drug dealer who also murdered people for a living. By now my circle of friends was a far stretch from the ones I had grown up with. However, I came to know Jessie—the Jessie who cared, who cried, and who had a heart.

I was at one of his crack houses when he came in to pick up the money and drop off the drugs. His demeanor was interesting and intriguing. He noticed me staring at him and said, "Why you looking at me like that…Do you know me or something?"

"No I don't, but you remind me of someone," I replied.

He reminded me of my daddy. Yeah, I can see how my mother was attracted to my dad and drawn into this lifestyle. These men had money, swag and were considered bad boys. And for some reason, women are attracted to those kinds of men.

"Why you here, you get high off this stuff?" he asked.

"Yeah, I do," I replied.

"Wow! You don't look like the girls I'm used to seeing around here," he said. "You busy?"

"Am I busy, he got jokes!", I thought.

He continued, "You know what, I need you to come take a ride with me." He caught me off guard, because remember he's a killer and if I say no what would he do?

"Ok," I said. I was scared out of my mind and didn't want to go without getting another hit. But then I thought, *"Tanya go! He has the drugs."*

I got into his clean and shiny black Range Rover with tinted windows; the sounds were bumping. I hadn't heard good music in such a long time. He drove to a store on Detroit's east side and told the owner to hook me up. The next thing I knew, I had on a fresh pair of jeans, a beautiful floral top and a brand new pair of boots. Then the owner brought out a navy blue ski jacket with a matching hat and scarf. I remember Jessie saying "Put it on my tab, man."

We left there and went to a small restaurant where they served vegetarian food. In the back of my mind I was thinking, *"Is this what they do before they kill you...clothe and feed you first?"*

We walked in, me trailing behind him as he ordered the food. We then walked over to a little table in the back corner of the restaurant where he handed me a sandwich off the tray and asked, "Do you like vegetarian food?"

I said, "Never tried it."

"It's good for you," he replied.

His phone rung; I couldn't hear the conversation, but while I was eating I thought to myself, *"Why is he doing all this? What is his motive?"* He hadn't shared his reasoning with me yet.

As he got off the phone he asked, "You like the sandwich?"

I replied, "It's pretty good I must say."

"Well I guess you're wondering why I asked you to come with me, huh."

"Yes," I replied thinking, *"that's an under-statement at this point."*

"I saw this innocent girl." He continued, "And like I said, you didn't look like the other girls I was used to seeing around, so I felt I needed to rescue you..." He laughed and continued, "You need to go home! Where do you live?" he asked.

"On the west side, "I answered.

"Well I'm taking you home," he said.

"No don't do that!" I told him. "I'll just come back, if not your spot someone else's."

"How did you get hooked on crack?" he asked.

"Can you believe L.A., with the Stars," I replied.

"You been to L.A.?" he asked.

"Yes, I had dreams of becoming a star, an actress, but all I became was a 'rock star' get it," We laughed. "No, I'm not kidding. I wanted to be on the soap operas, a movie star," I replied.

"You know what, I had dreams too," he said.

"You did." I replied.

"Yes, I always wanted to sing."

"Oh really, let me hear you."

He began to sing a tune from *Boys II Men* and he sounded really good.

"You really can sing," I began laughing… "I haven't laughed like this in a long time Jessie. Thanks! Thanks for everything. Anybody else know you sing like this?" I asked.

"No and you bet not say anything either," he replied.

People didn't know this side of Jessie. They didn't know that he didn't even like what he was doing anymore, but he was in too deep, knew too much, and couldn't get out. We would talk about me getting off drugs and him wanting to quit the business, all the time. When together we were different people than the way our world perceived us. We built a really nice relationship in spite of our lifestyle.

He had the money that's for sure and the drugs as well. What was interesting is how he wouldn't let me smoke crack, but I could do a few lines of coke, which was not my drug of choice –that he didn't mind. Jessie began to gain trust, which allowed me to ride around with him to all his joints. I had moved up from being a drug addict to drug dealer's girl-friend with an addiction on the side.

It was 2:00 A.M., and Jessie had been out at the club with his buddies all night. I received a call from one of his friends saying, "Jessie was rushed to the hospital, he's been shot twenty-three times." I was startled by what I had just heard because Jessie was the killer, never the victim. But I was very happy when they assured me he was going to survive.

The recovery process was overwhelming. When he returned home from the hospital I took good care of him: changing his bloody bandages, feeding him, bathing him, and caring for him until he was able to do for himself.

Being with Jessie offered a new and exciting frontier to explore and conquer. A lot of money began to come through my hands and he purchased a lot of nice things for me—especially for being right by his side. My life was now the saying, "Having my cake and eating it too." I was looking decent, and people were respecting me because I was Jessie's girl. Eventually, my addiction was bound to kick into fifth gear being around the amount of drugs he allowed me to handle...What I became was a dressed up mess.

Did I mention that Jessie was a ladies' man, a player? He had several women. Most of the crack houses were owned by the women he had relations with. At the time, I thought an "open" relationship would be considered the "bomb." I could do what I wanted to do and he could do what he wanted to do. When Jessie was with these other women I would get high. I started dipping into the sack of cocaine, taking out a little bit at a time, then try to fix it back so it would look like it hadn't been tampered with. I would add flour to it to keep the weight the same. The only thing wrong with this, the complaints were starting to stream in about the strength of his cocaine; it was getting weaker and weaker.

The night Jessie came home and I was trying to hide what I was doing. That night I really wanted him to leave like he normally would because my addiction was overwhelming me. We were upstairs in the bedroom doing the usual talking and socializing. I would tell him I had to go to the bathroom. Quickly, I'd walk towards the bathroom, and sneak downstairs. Hit the pipe, come back upstairs and go in the bathroom to get myself together, brushed my teeth and walked back in the bedroom like nothing ever happened. I did that about four times that night until I stayed too long.

He had dozed off to sleep, or so I thought. I had to mix and cook up the crack again; I was out of the first batch I had fixed. At the same time he came downstairs wondering where I was. Startled, he asked, "What are you doing?"

Calmly, I played it off, "I'm warming some water to fix me some tea."

Afterwards we went back upstairs to watch TV, and when I saw him doze off again, I got up and went back downstairs to finish what I was doing. I wanted it bad, nothing mattered to me but reaching the peak of my high over and over again. While I was in my element he woke up, saw that I wasn't in bed, came downstairs and caught me in the act.

Stunned, he asked, "What in the hell you doing? I can't believe that you're doing this to yourself again. When did you start back smoking crack? Why Tanya, why…"

I was so embarrassed and responded frantic, "I don't know, I don't know."

"How much do you have? Is this it?" He asked.

"This is it," I replied.

He started searching the house and went through everything. He broke the pipe, put it in a paper bag and took it outside to the garbage dumpster. Then he found some of what I had hidden and he flushed it down the toilet. He was so angry; I had not seen this side of Jessie before. I heard about it but I hadn't seen him in action. The first thing that went through my head was, *"Is he going to kill me or physically abuse me?"*

I had no clue of what was about to happen, but the one thing still on my agenda was getting high. He told me to come upstairs with him. We got back in bed and I laid beside him wondering what was next. His silence was killing me. But he fell back to sleep and because of what just occurred, I really wanted another hit. I got out of bed, snuck back downstairs, went outside, climbed into the dumpster and got the broken pipe. I came back in the house and feverishly tried to fix the pipe so I could numb my pain. Then I went in the basement searching through the sack again. I stood trembling, trying to cook another batch using a lighter this time. Well, he wasn't as sound asleep as I had originally thought. He came looking and when he found me in the basement, I panicked! We struggled back and forth as he ripped the pipe from my hands. That's when I grabbed the knife that I had used to open the package of cocaine.

He froze looking at me confused and disgusted. I knew I should not have done that. He said, "What, you trying to kill me over this s%$#? It's time for me to go before I kill you girl! I want you the hell out of here by the time I come back. B*#@#! You hear me!"

He cleaned house before he left. He took all the money and the drugs with him. I asked myself, *"Why can't I stop doing this? I want help, but I also want to get high more than anything."*

I left the house searching. The drugs would make my problems disappear. I didn't think it made new problems. I was very confused. My dreams had been shattered, my hopes and expectations crushed. I asked myself, *"Is anything important to me anymore?"*

Nothing was important—not my family, my friends,

and right now not even me. Yet, for the first time I started questioning *God*. I wondered where he was and why I didn't feel his presence in my life. Ordinarily, grandmother did all the praying.

"Now it's just me and you *God!* Where did you go?"

Had he abandoned me or had I abandoned him? "I'm sorry *God*. If ever there was a time I needed you, it is **NOW!**"

I prayed to *God* asking for him to come and change my life back to the way it used to be. And if I had a choice of where I'd like to go, it would be right back to the competitions in the Nationals. I was so happy then. I had no worries, no relationships and I wasn't an *Addict*. I was enjoying life on my own terms, not crack's! Or if ever there was a moment when I wanted to turn back the time and crawl back into my mother's womb and start all over, **THIS WAS IT...**

Two weeks after Jessie had kicked me out, I was getting high at a crack house on Farnsworth Street that Dray introduced me to. I overheard others saying that Jessie had been shot and killed; two bullets to the head. Supposedly Jessie killed one of the guy's brothers. I didn't want to believe what I was hearing. Just a couple of weeks ago I lived with this man, and now he's dead? I had known of his prior lifestyle, but that wasn't his profession while we were together. At least not that I knew of. Would he have kept things like that away from me? No matter what, Jessie was good to me. I messed things up. Wow! What if I had been with him that night? What if he didn't tell me to leave? Was my life spared because *God* had spared it with his loving grace, or was this my destiny...but why Jessie?

He who is pregnant with evil and conceives trouble gives birth to disillusionment. He who digs a hole and scoops it out falls into a pit he has made. The trouble he caused recoils on himself, his violence comes down on his own head...

Psalms 7:13-16

I continued for weeks getting high at the same crack house, and to make matters worse I didn't even attend Jessie's funeral. My addiction was of greater importance than to respect the dead or his family. Matter of fact, I didn't have much respect for anyone...not even myself.

CHAPTER EIGHT

While prostituting my body, I also was in on store robberies as the lookout and the bag girl, all to support my habit. I would go into stores with boosters who stole items and would be the one who carried the items out of the store in a bag. This was another source of means to getting high. But It was only a matter of time before I'd get caught...While in Hudson's Department Store located inside the mall, security tapped me on my shoulder and told me to come with them. It appeared they had me on camera. I had a bag filled with two designer outfits by clothing designer's Donna Karan and Escada worth thirty-five hundred dollars. These items on the street were worth about fifteen hundred dollars.

This is how it works: The booster would sell to a person who was known as a "fence" for one-third of the actual price. In turn, the "fence" would sell the merchandise on the street for half the ticket price, and I would receive from the booster one-hundred to one-hundred and fifty measly dollars to support my habit.

This was my first offense, so I was released on a personal bond and set free with the intent to come back on my court date. Now, if I couldn't make the funeral what would make me think I would return to court?

Later that year, I was picked up on a warrant for not showing up in court for that shoplifting offense. I was sent to the county jail and locked up behind bars for six months. The realization of my life began to unravel my world. When those bars go click, click, the person you call is not your mother, granddaddy, or your grandmother; it is *God*. Now, I would have all the time in the world for *Him*. I began to explore the Bible, discovering many things about the Lord that I did not know. I learned that if I repented for my sins and mistakes he would be faithful and would forgive me.

But if we confess our sins to him, he is faithful and just to forgive us and our sins and to cleanse us from all unrighteousness...

1 John 1:9

I began to make many promises to *GOD* that I didn't think I could ever keep. I had already promised my grandparents and let them down. I promised my mother too. And now I was promising *GOD*. Would I let him down too? That was the real question.

Do not break your oath, but keep the oaths you have made to the Lord. But I tell you, do not swear at all: either by heaven, for it is GOD's throne: or by the earth for it is his footstool: or by Jerusalem, for it is the city of the Great King. And do not swear by your head, for you cannot make even one hair white or black. Simply let your "Yes" be "Yes" and your "No" be "No"...

Matthew 5:33-37

When I returned home from jail I was released to my mother's house, where I would live and finish the remaining two years of my probation. By this time my mother had purchased a home of her own, and I was very happy for her; this was something she always wanted.

Mother was so happy to have me home with her. She longed for me to be clean and sober and safe. My mother always wanted what most mothers wanted for their children, a calm, normal, healthy lifestyle that hopefully included grandchildren someday. A wish I hadn't been able to fulfill for her considering that I had had eight abortions while being in the streets. But this time, I believed I was ready for the task and ready to begin the journey towards clean and sober living.

It was Monday morning; I was sitting on the front porch relaxing and reading an Essence Magazine. It was a hot summer day with a cool breeze blowing slowly. I had just completed a pedicure on my feet and painted my toenails red. While waiting for my toes to dry, a young man approached me on the porch.

"Hi, I live down the street, the second house from the corner. I've been seeing you from time to time," he said, and continued. "I was wondering, what's your name?"

"Tanya," I replied.

"Well Tanya, my name is Paris, pleased to meet you. You look like you're enjoying this sunny afternoon."

"Yes I am." I answered.

"Well I'm not going to keep you. Maybe we can have lunch one day; I'll make something special…Get to know one another since we're neighbors," he replied.

"Maybe," I said to him. All the while knowing I wanted to say yes to this fine handsome young man. But I played it safe, wanting to get to know him first, trying a different approach for a change. I definitely didn't need another married man or a drug dealer in my life…or killer either.

"Leave me your number, I'll call you," I said to him.

"By the way I love red toes," he mentioned, with a grin on his face. I looked down at my feet forgetting I had just painted them red.

"Thanks, I said thinking, *"hmmm he's a cutie."*

Paris was a few years younger than I was. I just felt

after all I had been through he might be just a little wet behind the ears for me. Paris was a light skinned black man, gorgeous, and well-built. I was thinking he had to be a mixed race because his hair had the texture of a white male's hair. He wasn't as tall as I preferred him to be, but he was fine and his name fit him well. Paris was definitely a smooth talker, and very persistent. You know the type that was used to getting whatever he wanted, and usually got it. He was smart, intelligent and a Christian. Paris would talk a lot about the Lord and often I would find him reading his Bible. He was very different from the men I was accustomed to. But I was considered "Street," an "Addict"...*I don't think he really ever saw that coming.*

Paris and I began to have lots of fun together. I'm sure being friends first gave us a secure foundation for a future. Our dating consisted of picnics, long walks, movies and friendly chats. As we got better acquainted, he began to share his past with me and some things I could relate to very well. Paris had never drank, smoked or did any drugs of any kind, but his mother Katherine was a different story. Katherine had experienced prostitution and did some jail time for selling drugs to support her household. In some of our conversations he would say I reminded him of his mother, and as our relationship continued I eventually met her.

A friend I met after high school named Tasha and I would attend a male review sometimes on weekends. There were two well-known clubs around back then, one was "Watts Mozambique" and the other, "Henry's Lounge." The male review consisted of guys who formed groups and made up dance routines to songs by the Whispers, the O' Jays, the Four Tops, the Temptations and Men at work-YMCA. They would mock these groups in dance and sensually turn the clubs out. The guys who were dancing were built, fine, sexy, and paid in full. Ladies would bring hundreds of dollars to stick into their G-strings or tape dollar bills together and form lines to give money to them like they were Kings.

At the time, Paris was manager at Pizza Hut right around the corner from where we lived and he was about to be laid off from his job, due to cut backs. Paris was a good dancer and had the body that was needed to be considered in a male review. I suggested to him that he should come with me to "Watts" or "Henry's" one evening so I could show him something, never revealing that I thought this would be a perfect job for him.

One Friday night, we went to "Watts"; the club was packed. Paris couldn't believe how many women were crammed into this club and freely giving their money away to these attractive male dancers. I think seeing the concept really excited him, and knowing it was legal, was even better. After the club closed, I took Paris to the dressing room in the back to meet some of the fellas. They were celebrities in their profession, and plenty of women would stay after the show to take pictures with them. This was yet another source of income. The dancers and the photographer would split the profits fifty-fifty. I think at that point Paris saw the same dollar signs as I did, and the guys quickly welcomed him.

Immediately, Paris started meeting up with them for rehearsals. When he began to dance, I would go to support and watch him make all his money. The women fell in love with him...Instantly! Along with his looks, he had a smile out of this world and that's all it took to rake in the cash.

During this time, his mother Katherine and I became very fond of each other. Katherine treated me like I was one of her own, and of course, I knew what she did for a living. Yet I admired her strength and her ability to run this type of business as a woman and at the same time take good care of her household. It was always something about women with strength I admired; and from what I heard and seeing her now, gave me hope of taking control of my life back. At this point I had been clean a little over a year and only one year of probation left.

One Friday afternoon, I was visiting Paris's home. Paris was taking a shower preparing for his evening job, while Katherine and I were sitting in the kitchen. She was cooking their dinner, and I was getting some pointers, when a customer of hers came by to purchase a supply of crack. She knew about my addiction and would not do any transactions in front of me. She and her client, Pearl, continued down into her basement where she would allow her preferred clients to smoke. Katherine had a sophisticated clientele. They were teachers, nurses, factory workers and other working class people—people we call *"Functional Addicts."* She didn't sell to street addicts because her clients were coming to purchase crack where she and her children actually lived.

The phone rang, and I went downstairs to hand the call to her and I noticed that Pearl had the pipe fired up. At the same time the doorbell rang and Katherine proceeded up the stairs to answer it, leaving me downstairs alone with Pearl. Pearl was a nurse that worked at one of Detroit's largest hospitals and during her lunch break she would get high. Pearl left abruptly, rushing back to work but seemed to leave something behind. There were crumbs left lying on the table…

Yet the dogs under the table eat of the children's crumbs…

Mark 7:28

Katherine was still up stairs and the pipe seemed to be calling me saying, "Just one hit." The voice within me wouldn't stop. It kept nagging me, "Come on, just one." I thought for that sudden moment of the euphoric rush exploding inside of my head just sitting there waiting for me to light up! There was already smoke left inside the bowl of the pipe which was still hot. But I needed to run up the stairs quickly. Instantly, I wrapped my hands around the crack pipe in the vain hope of deflecting what was about to come, and I fired up. *"Oh God, I promised I wouldn't."*

What did I do? Why can't I do what I say I'm going to do…?

I blew the smoke out my mouth quickly. I heard Katherine coming back downstairs. I rushed into the bathroom flushing the toilet, trying to get myself together; looking in the mirror in shame. *"What would they say if they found out what I just did?"* I thought to myself. Paris had not seen me this way, my cover would be blown. I couldn't fool them for very long, even I knew now…*I wouldn't stay clean much longer.*

I came out of the bathroom as if I had done nothing wrong. "Pearl said she'd be back after work. I'm going home to change; please tell Paris I'll call him later," I said to Katherine as I left the house.

What had I done to deserve a life of such continuing struggle?

That evening, I was driving to see Paris dance at "Henry's." On my way, I heard that strong voice within me again that seemed to always surface. *"Go left, make a quick stop and get one hit, just one."* I had a clear recollection of a traumatic experience coming upon me. I knew if I made that quick left, my life was bound to take a turn for the worst. Did I think about the consequences? *Not really.* Did I think about my relationship? *No.* Paris was a good man. But I talked myself into believing I was fine and he'd never find out. *"This will just take a moment and afterwards I'll go right to the club to see him dance and everything will be just fine,"* I told myself that over and over.

CHAPTER NINE

I arrived at one of my favorite spots, Farnsworth Street. I knew it was always open and product would be flowing. I rushed to the door in a hurry to get to my final destination to see Paris dance. I quickly asked the guy, "What you got, any nickels? Come on, I'm in a hurry." I walked towards the back where the others were getting high, but I didn't see any familiar faces in the room. It was normal for me to know someone, so I could use their pipe to smoke my crack with. I asked some girl who had sat her pipe down on the table if I could use it. This was the customary way addicts introduced themselves to other addicts. She said to me, "Sure, but you have to share with me." Of course, I said yes…*In this addiction world nothing comes free.* As I lit the torch and pulled really hard, I held on to the smoke as long as I could. When I blew out, automatically the fear that I was worthless surfaced again. Obviously, I shouldn't have been surprised, I deserved it. Here I was once more in this vicious cycle of insanity.

Insanity: Thinking I can do the same thing over and over again and expect different results.

Nothing was different. Not even the high itself, not the *people, nor the places, or the things.* Why did I think I could leave after doing one hit? I continuously fooled myself into thinking this could happen—then desperately wanting someone to hurt me, not help me; that way I could always use it as my excuse.

The verdict of my life was out and the conclusion was if I took my life, this addiction would be over. But I didn't have the guts to do that either. Alarmed by my thoughts, I continued to get high for days. I was so scared to surface back from the dead once again. I knew I had let so many people down and now I had added Paris to my list; knowing that night he would be worried out of his mind wondering what had happened to me. Yet I'm sure his own sensibility would eventually kick in and he'd realize where I was and what I was doing—*she must be getting high...*

Three weeks passed like time was standing still. I was very good at hiding from everyone while getting high. On my way to cop I began to feel very nauseous and started vomiting all over the sidewalks. Having money in my pocket or health insurance in my wallet never crossed my mind. It was only me and crack; my best friend, my love and right now my god.

You shall have no other gods before me. You shall not make for yourself an idol in the form of anything in heaven above or on the earth beneath or in the waters below, you shall not bow down to them or worship them; for I, the Lord your GOD, am a jealous GOD...

Exodus 20:3-5

As I was debating whether to keep going to the crack house I stumbled across a clinic. This clinic was packed with people that looked just like me—dirty, smelly, homeless alcoholics and addicts that needed to be checked out for various reasons. I scurried through the door to find out what was wrong with me. It could have been anything, but I knew whatever it was, it wasn't good. The clinic was drab, dirty, and uninviting. As I sat in the reception area, I signed under an assumed name, not admitting my true identity.

Upon being called into the examining room, the doctor came in shortly to examine me. The examination was short and sweet, a little blood drawn and I was asked to pee in a cup. The doctor returned saying, "I have good news; you're nine weeks pregnant."

"Pregnant," I replied to him.

Tears sprang from my eyes and my heart nearly fell to my feet. I didn't know what I expected to hear but it definitely wasn't those words that just came out of his mouth. Oh my God! It's Paris' baby. All I could think about was the amount of drugs I had consumed and the effects that it would have on our baby. I certainly didn't want to consider going back home. I couldn't handle any disappointment—the criticism, my failures—and besides I didn't even know if Paris wanted me anymore. The wheel of fear reactivated all over again. The thought of being rejected by anyone, especially Paris, was too much to bear. What if he didn't want the baby or worse, what if he didn't want to have anything to do with me? Here I was with more emotional stress and the only way I knew how to relieve it was to get high…

I knew the recycling of this unhealthy behavior was not the answer. I needed to go home, no right or left turns, just straight to my mother's house. Why couldn't I do this simple task? Not a simple task for a crack addict. I know it seems so easy, but "Crack" isn't easy, it won't take "NO" for an answer. I would pause momentarily, confused, but somehow crack always *won*…

Within hours I was copping crack again. While walking towards the back of the crack house, minutes later the police rushed in, raiding the place. We were all scattering everywhere. The police read us all our rights, handcuffed us and took us straight to the precinct for booking. When they ran my fingerprints, they discovered I had a warrant out for my arrest. I had missed reporting to my probation officer. This time I was held without bond, because I was in violation of my current charge.

The next morning I stood before the judge as he sentenced me to five months in the county jail—the rest of the time I had left on my probation—and added an additional two more years of probation. There I was sitting in a concrete cell with a toilet, sink, metal bed and a blow up mattress. I was put on special attention because of my pregnancy and was taken out to the hospital every month for check-ups.

A month later, I finally wrote to my mother to make her aware of where I was and explained my pregnancy. She immediately wrote back to me expressing her excitement about the baby and of course, she mentioned this information to my family and Paris.

Before long, while I was sleeping in my cell, an officer came, "Tanya Harp, you have a visitor."

I jumped up quickly. I stood there for a moment, and asked "Who is it?"

She hadn't a clue. My heart was beating fast. I couldn't imagine who it was. Was it Granddaddy, my mother or Paris? Walking down the long hallway the entanglement of what I was about to face was heightened. I was put into a visiting cell with a bullet proof glass window and a phone. I sat directly facing the chair on the other side. There was silence for a moment. I'm sure my face was covered with a look of defeat with my heart beating faster and faster. *"Say something!"* I thought to myself.

Slowly he raised his head and nodded for me to pick up the phone.

"How are you doing?" he said.

"I'm fine," I replied.

"You taking care of yourself?" he asked.

"Yes, the best that I can in here," I answered.

"How's the baby," he spoke softly.

"She's fine," I replied.

"Oh, you know what we're having," he said.

"Yes Paris, it's a girl."

Even though Paris was not the type of guy that made you feel worse than what I already felt. To spare myself further humiliation I just began speaking in a remorseful and apologetic way, promising that this wouldn't happen again.

"I will not be doing anymore drugs," I assured him. "The baby is healthy according to the doctors, and I don't want to put the baby in any more danger." I also mentioned to him that I had two more months left in jail and that I would be seven months pregnant by the time I was released.

Paris visited continuously, reassuring me that he'd be right by my side. I had a great support system. My mother and grandparents made sure I had everything I needed to take good care of myself and the baby, and the women in jail would save their milk so I would have plenty.

When I returned to my mother's home, she and Paris had planned a baby shower. There were so many gifts, that I and the baby didn't want for anything. Many of my mother's and Paris` friends and family attended, not many of my friends because most were addicts. I was thrilled to be back to realization. As always, my life seemed to be back to normal. I felt loved and connected to my family and Paris was such a proud father. His mom was excited about the baby too. It was a very happy time for all of us...

I was clean and sober; eating all the right foods, doing what was best for my baby; determined to change the direction of my life. Periodically, I would get a little depressed, but at least I didn't care to use.

On May 6, 1985, I gave birth to a beautiful girl. Paris named her Parisia Le`Marie Harp. Her middle name was derived from a combination of both our middle names. We danced around the subject of marriage, actually discussing it a lot along with other things after the baby was born.

Weeks after Parisia was born Paris wanted to talk to me about something important. I was excited that he might be ready to pop the big question, so I quickly went to his house to see him, not knowing what to expect. Unfortunately, the news was quite shocking and I didn't quite understand...

"Tanya, I have to tell you what's going on with me," he said.

"What do you mean," I replied.

"Tanya I have a calling on my life and I've answered it."

"What kind of calling Paris?" I asked.

"I'm going into the ministry to become a Minister," he continued. "I won't be dancing anymore."

The first thing that came to my mind was, *Wow! I definitely wouldn't fit the image of a first lady.* "When did this happen?" I asked.

"A couple of weeks ago, I struggled with the issue a little and I didn't know how to tell you."

What do you say after hearing something like this? Do I ask the man to choose me over *God?* Even as an addict I knew better than that. Yet I accepted his decision as naturally as I could.

My resistance to change was a symptom of how strong a hold fear had on me. I knew I wasn't ready for this lifestyle. I didn't believe that my addiction was completely gone. I was just waiting for it to surface like it always had. But things were different now; I loved Paris and our baby. In addition to my feelings and thoughts, how could I truly live up to all the expectations? Casting doubt on all I had been telling him...

"Can I have a day to think all this over?" I asked him.

"Sure baby, I know this may be a bit much and a big switch from where our relationship started. But it's something I have to do, I have no choice," he continued. "I love you and Parisia dearly and she'll be attending church with me, if you decide you're not ready. I can't make you do anything you don't want to do, you're a grown woman. But, I am responsible for my child. She is going to know Jesus," he said.

"I know Jesus," I replied.

"Do you really? Do you really know what he's capable of doing? *God* can instantly turn you around, that's what he did for me and he can do it for you, if you just trust and believe in him Tanya."

Why did it seem so easy for him? Why couldn't I just get it right and get it quickly?

There were decisions to be made. I knew I couldn't ponder for long; he was serious and ready for change. My intentions were strong but unfortunately my actions—as usual I always neglected them to accomplish my task. Things went smoothly for a while at first, but as quickly and quietly as I could, I would be gone before he knew it. Subconsciously, I lived in constant awareness of my disposition...

Chapter Ten

I was home with the baby napping, while my mom was at work and Paris was attending ministry school at his church, when the phone rang. I rushed to answer it; it was Dray on the other end. He was calling because a friend of his had just received a new package and wanted some of his friends to try things out. He explained that he had just run across my number and was really trying to see if the number was still working. My mother had always kept the same number unfortunately.

I whispered to him, "I have my baby and no one is here to watch her right now."

He didn't care; he wanted me to know he and others were there smoking. I hung up the phone terrified. I wanted to leave right then, especially since it was on him for a change. I was due a freebie; I had supported most of our binges. But there was no one available to watch Parisia. I sat there trying to figure out what to do, whether or not to take her with me. My addiction was starting to stir up inside of me just knowing it was available and free. The unmistakable command of the voice within said, *"Go! Go!"*

Right then and there, like I didn't have a care in the world, I packed up Parisia in a lovely pink blanket, grabbed a bottle of milk out of the refrigerator and ran straight for my car. I was driving about ninety miles per hour to get there fast. I pulled up to Dray's house, got out, and grabbed Parisia from the back seat with her in one hand and my purse in the other. I bolted towards the door. I knew I didn't have much time, and I needed to get back home without any of them knowing we had ever left.

I knocked relentlessly, pounding on the door until someone answered; a young man opened the door, asking me, "What do you want," staring at my baby in my hands. Dray overheard and said, "Who is it man?"

I looked over the man's shoulder and said, "It's me Dray, Tanya!

Dray came to the door with his mouth filled with crack smoke. As he greeted me he connected his lips to mine and blew the smoke into my mouth from his. Immediately, my legs became weak and shaky. I sat Parisia down in the car seat in the corner of the room next to the couch. I gave her a bottle to keep her quiet and went to work.

Watching the others consume what was about to be an explosive high, I couldn't wait my turn. They passed me the plate of those precious stones. I loaded up the pipe, flicked the lighter and inhaled deeply. I passed the pipe to someone else and awaited my turn again. I loaded the pipe again flicked the lighter and as soon as I inhaled, Parisia began to cry. I took the lighter and lit the pipe again and again. Her crying was growing louder and louder. By this time the smoke filled the room with a dense fog. When I looked over towards her, I couldn't see through it. They were all yelling for me to "shut her ass up." At that moment, I didn't care. I grabbed another precious stone; I knew this was going to be my last hit, because they were ready to put me out. I inhaled and held on tight to the ultimate sensation of my high. The crying continued sounding like thunder, then all of a sudden I heard nothing...silence.

I dropped the pipe and screamed, "Where's my baby, where is my baby!"

When I found her it appeared that she wasn't breathing, she wouldn't open her eyes. What had I done? I turned and saw the table on fire. Someone had spilled rum and a burning candle fell on top. I panicked! I became so paranoid that the high had me tripping. It was like the entire place was on fire. I grabbed Parisia wrapped in a pink blanket that now looked red. *God* forbid was she on fire too? I went running out the front door, screaming, "My baby's dead, I killed her!"

I put Parisia in the car, not knowing what to do. I thought, *"I'll go the house. My mother will help me. She'll know."* If I took her to the hospital, I would have been doomed to get arrested. It was by the grace of *God* that I made it to the house. As I pulled up, my mother was sitting on the porch. She could see that something was wrong. I was screaming and crying as I approached her, "I killed her Momma! I killed her."

"What have you done?" she asked, grabbing Parisia out of my hands. "Baby calm down," she said.

She looked at Parisia holding her in her arms, and said, "Hey grandma's precious girl."

"Momma, is she alright?"

"Yes! She's fine," she answered, and continued in rage. "Tanya, you got to get some help. This is not normal actions of a mother. How stupid can you be to do something like this? I've tried and tried, time after time to understand the hold this drug has over you."

"Momma, I'm sorry, I'm so sorry," I cried. "I know I'm not a good mother to her. I took her to the crack house Momma, how could I have done this to my baby. What kind of mother does this?"

"I don't know, but you need to get help! Baby, this could have turned out worse than it did, you drove up like a bat out of hell. But I'm telling you right now, don't involve this baby again, you hear me!"

I admitted my transgression fully, expecting to be confronted by my mother. I knew Paris would be outraged when he found out also. When he confronted me I didn't have much to say. I was shattering the conveyed, one on one conversation, constantly betraying him. I would mouth the words with desperation but without sincerity. You could tell that he didn't believe a word I was saying. I didn't even wait for his reply; I just hung up the phone.

I knew this was it. I threw myself into a situation where I had very few options left. Before this had happened I thought I had finally made some progress, but maybe I expected too much too soon. I knew they all meant well, but they didn't understand. They could never understand. I was an addict, a person who hadn't any understanding myself. *I was powerless over this addiction...*

CHAPTER ELEVEN

CRACK was on the rise. Drug dealers had taken over many single family homes and apartments located in an area they renamed "The Dead End." The apartment building I frequently visited was called "Grand Central Station", very similar to the "Carter" in the movie, "New Jack City." The dealers and users would use some of the units for smoking crack and some for sexual activities. The dealers would actually hold the residents hostage by using iron gates to gate them off in a small section of their own homes. Most residents were crack addicts themselves and received crack as payment for occupying their residence.

These drug dealers were ruthless. They cared about no one, not even their own mothers. They sold to anyone and everyone, all they cared about was the root of all evil, "Money."

Two well-known guys in that area controlled 118 crack houses—63 were dime joints and 55 were nickel joints. These locations were open 24/7 and were very busy with traffic. Someone could have gotten the impression that maybe the police were involved since there were no arrests made, nor were the houses even being raided during this time. This particular building was located near a church. I would sit on the step of this church, high out of my mind never recognizing that it was actually a church. I would squat for hours at a time when I was tired or trying to figure out how I was going to get my next hit.

A year had passed. I hadn't seen my grandparents, my mother, Paris or Parisia—the people who meant the world to me. I wondered from time to time what they were doing; always trying to picture what Parisia looked like. Did she look like me or her father? What was she like? I had heard from my cousin Daryl who I saw in passing, that my family was ready to pronounce me dead. I wasn't dead; however, I felt like the walking dead...

Now I was living in a two-family flat; lying on the floor, cold. Downstairs was where I would cop and upstairs was where I smoked my crack. The place had no electricity, no running water or gas. Candles were the only form of light and there was a kerosene heater for heat. This place was filthy, with a couple of old blankets lying around, but to us this was a five-star hotel. This particular night we were doing the usual, when the place caught on fire. This was the second time there was a fire around me while I was getting high. We ran for our lives, scattering without alternatives, with only one exit, it was chaos. I and a few others were able to escape, but there were three others that were found dead. The fire trucks and police didn't respond quickly in this area to these situations. And by the time they did arrive, the duplex had completely burned to the ground. Every time from that point on when I got high, I thought I was on fire. I felt like the enemy {Satan} used this as a way to torture and torment me. Really, he {Satan} was using against me the very thing he had used to entice me.

The thief does not come except to kill, steal, and destroy...

John 10:10

When I now would fire up the pipe, all I would see was fire. Now many would think this would be a good time to quit. But do you think I considered that? Absolutely not, my addiction was not easily broken nor was the lifestyle that came along with it.

Shortly after, the drug dealers started making serious bets with one another while they watched me go through this fire ordeal.

"Man you want to see something funny as hell, give her one." He would say. "This is going to blow your mind."

The drug dealer would hand me one of those precious stones. I would place the whole rock on the pipe and fire it up, consuming all of it in one pull—sending me straight into orbit.

I'd grab hold of the person standing closest to me and actually blow on them like they were on fire. I would run behind things trying to hide from the fire. Certain colors like red, yellow, or orange would increase my crazy out of control behaviors even more. When I came down from the high I would return back to normal, wanting another hit as if nothing had ever happened.

Their response would be, "You have to be crazy as hell for wanting anymore after what I just saw."

But I didn't care; I was ready to take that ride to hell again. I even remember thinking, *"if I could just get through the first one without blasting off, maybe I could receive a second one for free, and therefore I wouldn't have to have sex for it."* This thinking reminded me of something in Proverbs...

There is a way that seems right to man, but its end is the way to death...

Proverbs14:2

"This time I'll try my hardest to get through the first one," I told myself.

"Man nothing happened, what's up," he said.

"Man, give her one more, she's about to take off," he replied.

It all became a game to them, but the game was at my expense. One thing was for sure, I definitely wasn't able to make it through the second one to receive a third one. I'm 5 feet 4 inches tall and at the time I weighed about 105lbs, the combination of the substance and the adrenaline rush I would feel would cause my strength to increase. It reminded me of the power that *God* gave Samson with his extraordinary strength. But this wasn't any godly power I was experiencing. When I experienced those paranoid fire episodes, I could move a person weighing three hundred pounds or better out of my way. This only became something else for the drug dealers to bet on and for me to receive another free…

"Man, bet she can move the guy right there," he said.

"Man ain't no way that buck-o-five girl gone move him, you crazy, Bet!" the guy replied.

"She can't move me man, be for real," the guy himself would say.

After they had given me the second rock, not only did I move the guy that weighed three hundred pounds but anything else standing in the way of me getting away from this imaginary fire.

I ran straight out the house right into the traffic-filled street, where there were tons of cars moving in both directions. Witnesses told me when I was in the street running through traffic, they couldn't believe that not one car hit me. Cars were pressing on brakes, sliding a half mile before completely stopping. When I would finally calm down I'd come back inside asking for another hit, and they would say to each other, "Don't give her anything." It had gotten so out of control that the drug dealers didn't want me in their houses nor did they want my money anymore. I would have to go elsewhere, where they had no clue of how I reacted to the drug just to get high.

CHAPTER TWELVE

Meanwhile, many drug dealers themselves started getting high on their own supply. They would hang out in areas where no one was familiar with them. We call them "Functional borderline crack addicts" that eventually would fall by the wayside, because now they were coming up short of the money owed to their supplier.

One of those so-called dealers was a guy named Nathan, who I had met in passing. Nathan was also paranoid. He was obsessed with small white specks or lint, always thinking they were actual crack rocks. He would look around in carpet or pick lent off of any fabric, even off someone's clothing. This was his "Tweak" as we called it. I was on fire and he'd be on his knees searching for anything that looked like crack. It didn't matter whether he had crack or not, he still looked, and together, the two of us were what you call …"A hot mess."

One night after running out of crack, we drove to his house across town. As we entered his bedroom he said, "Make yourself at home." Nathan went into his closet and brought out a plate full of crack, telling me to help myself. As he handed me the pipe, I took the lighter, lit the pipe, inhaled, and blew the smoke out. That's when he spoke these words to me, "Did you know that you've been kidnapped? And your breakfast, lunch and dinner will be my d-i-c-k."

I thought I was dreaming, hoping to wake up quickly. This man and I had been getting high for at least three days together. Where did Mr. Hyde go? Who was this Dr. Jekyll …why didn't I see something like this coming? As he threw me down on the bed ripping my clothes off, and me fighting for my life. He grabbed my hands using them to flip me over. With my hands held behind my back he attempted to have anal sex with me. I screamed in agony; this was something I had never done before. He continued to push himself into me, hurting me further, I screamed at the top of my lungs, "Stop! Please stop, please, you're hurting me!"

I then asked, "Please can you get something, baby oil, Vaseline, lotion, something, please it hurts," I cried. "I can't take the pain anymore!"

He jumped up, leaving angrily to find something. At the same time I looked over at the window and noticed it was cracked open a bit. I lunged over, lifting it to climb out, and ran. I went running down an alley behind his house as fast as I could, not even realizing that I was naked; that's how terrified I was.

I cut between two houses until I was on the sidewalk, running past children that were playing outside. I ran onto a porch banging on the door as hard as I could. "Get off my porch!" she yelled.

"Lady please, help me!"

"Get off my porch before I call the police," she replied.

I proceeded running down the street to someone else's porch. I knocked relentlessly, until a woman answered. "Please help me, please," I said to her.

She turned to tell her husband, "Baby there's a naked lady on our porch."

He replied, "Baby don't just stand there, let her in."

They opened the door, having one of their children run

upstairs to get me something to cover up with. I began to explain to them what had just happened, telling them that I had been kidnapped and climbed out of a window to get away from the man who was attempting to rape me. The husband immediately called the police. Of course, I didn't give all the details.

While we were waiting for the police to arrive, the couple was very kind and understanding, offering me food. What was that? All I had been consuming was crack, cigarettes, and wild Irish rose. I hadn't eaten a meal in God knows when. They prepared a couple of hot dogs for me and a glass of kool-aid. You would have thought I was eating filet mignon with onions, and mushroom in rosemary cream sauce and a glass of wine.

When the police arrived, there were plenty of questions for the complaint report. The kind couple called me a cab and gave me twenty dollars. When the cab arrived, I thanked them for all they had done for me. I had given them the address to my mother's home and they told the driver where to drop me off.

While riding in the back of the cab, I was gazing out the window thinking, *"If only I could get just one more hit,"* Insane, huh? I was overcome with a disease called addiction. My first thought of course, was *"Tanya go home, this has to be enough,"* but there was always a voice that over powered my own. Why couldn't I just stick to my first thought? It's always been proven that the first choice is the right one. But I told the cab driver, "Turn left; I need to make a quick stop." I went right back to the same crack house where I met Nathan and began smoking crack all over again.

As a dog returns to its vomit, so a fool repeats his folly

Proverbs 26:11

Chapter Thirteen

I was coming out of the crack house with two other addicts, on our way to cop at another joint; the house we were at was all out. As we were stepping off the porch, they heard someone call out my name. "Tanya, I think that guy over there called you."

"Tanya, come here," I heard someone yell.

I turned to see who was calling me; it was Paris. Paris was standing before me in a black suit, with a crisp white shirt, red, black and white tie, black cashmere over coat and a black hat. He was looking like Billy D. Williams standing next to a silver Mercury Merkur XR4tI coupe. I stood there for a minute in shame, looking unkempt. I had cut off all my hair into a short afro and I had on someone else's borrowed jeans, t-shirt and coat. My clothes were battered and torn just like I was. Even my boots had holes in them; I was at my worst.

He said to me again, "Tanya, please come here."

I told the guys to go ahead; I'd catch up with them later. I walked towards Paris with such humiliation and hesitation. When I approached the car he asked, "Can you get in the car, I'll only be a moment."

I opened the door and got in hoping that the smell of me wouldn't hit him in the face. Paris had that passionate quality about him. It was part of who he was and it was his ministry. With my head held down almost into my lap he continued to ask me, "How are you doing?"

I replied, "I guess I'm alright."

"Look, I didn't come to force you to come home, I understand what you're dealing with, but I just needed to let you know that I love you, your mother and grandparents love you and your daughter needs you."

With my head still hanging down in shame, he took a picture out of his wallet and placed it in my hand. Tears began to fall from my eyes onto the picture of Parisia. She looked like a little princess dressed in a red and white polka-dotted dress sitting in an electric Barbie corvette. It was one of the things we had talked about getting her when we were together, and Paris had fulfilled one of my wishes for her.

I quickly handed him back the picture and said, "I can't even do it for her."

I felt worthless, hopeless, a failure as a mother, as a daughter, granddaughter and as a partner to him. I opened the door to the car, and said, "I have to go now."

His reply to me, "Take care of yourself and remember we love you."

I continued to walk back towards the crack house, without looking back. I could hear the car taking off slowly. I wanted to turn and scream "Wait, Wait for me!" But I wanted to take a hit on the pipe far more; secretly after seeing him and a picture of my beautiful daughter and what I gave up for crack, I was hoping the next hit would kill me. Death seemed easier than trying to walk back into their lives in shame.

The thing I couldn't understand was that what I was doing wasn't easy either. To be spoken down to, kidnapped, raped, and treated like a whore and told to do things like I was some dog begging—it wasn't easy either. I'm sure Paris mentioned to my mother my whereabouts, because a few days later my mother showed up.

I was in my element running the streets, which was now my home. That morning around 7:30 A.M. we were all smoking crack when there was a bang on the door. I heard someone ask, "Is my daughter Tanya here young man?"

He replied, "No lady you got the wrong house."

"No I got the right house and I'm not leaving until she comes to me."

At that moment I was so scared for her; these guys had no respect for life. They would shoot you for just looking at them the wrong way—I'd seen them do this before.

"Look lady we don't have no Tanya's here, I think you better leave."

What my mother didn't know was that I was now going by my street name, T-Baby, or Terrible-T. Only a couple of people knew my real name. The drug dealer came to the back room and said, "You got to go."

"No, tell her I'm not here," I said to him.

"You got to get the hell out of here, now!"

They snatched what was in my hands, grabbed me, and pulled me towards the door. My mother was standing there looking quite angry, but I could tell she was also glad to see my face. We left the porch and walked towards the car with her demanding that I get in. I felt like I was ten years old again and she was coming to get me from the playground after the street lights came on.

"Baby, come home, you look terrible," she said.

"Thanks Mom."

"No, look at you, why do you keep doing this to yourself? Do you know we wanted to pronounce you dead? What do I need to do? What can I do to help you?"

"Nothing Mom, every time I try to stay clean, I let everyone down." At that point I didn't even know why I was still getting high.

"Baby listen, *God* can help if you let him."

"Ma, No! *God* can't do anything…Where is he now, can't even help someone like me, I'm not a big job. So where is he Mother, where is he? Cause he's not here! He doesn't care about me or he would not have let this happen. Ma, I got to go."

"NO Tanya, if you get out of this car…"

"What Ma? Kill me, I'm already dead."

"That's not what I meant, Parisia needs her mother," she shouted.

"Ma you got what you wanted, you keep her. She's better off with you. I'll only take her with me to some crack house. This is my life; I intend to live in these streets till I die. I guess I'll quit then."

"Now you're talking crazy," she said.

"No Ma, just go and live your life, take care of Parisia and stop worrying about me. There's nothing you can do…"

"I can keep praying." She said.

CHAPTER FOURTEEN

"What My Mother Told Me"

With tears flowing down her cheeks, she never dreamed she would be sitting in her living room chair listening to every car that drove by. Running back and forth to the window wondering when her child was going to walk through the door. When the phone would ring, she'd stare at it for a couple of seconds before answering, deathly afraid to pick it up and hear someone say, "Mrs. Harp we have your daughter and we need you to come and identify her remains." What kind of mother wants to live like this daily? Not knowing where her child is or what's happening to her in the streets…

It's been two-years since I last saw or spoke to my daughter. I'd been praying every day and every night. I had her name on the altar at the church. I had the pastor and the congregation praying, my family, my friends, co-workers all praying and nothing. "Lord please bring her back to me," I asked *God* daily.

I was sure I was living my own life according to the word of the Lord. I gave, I loved, I honored my own mother and father, I loved my neighbors, and I was committed to my church. I sang in the choir, I helped feed the homeless, I extended my home or anything I had to anyone in need…I was becoming tired, many sleepless nights, caring for Parisia and working. Life was taking its toll on me.

I was on my way home from work. Paris had taken

Parisia with him, keeping her overnight. It was late that evening and I was extremely tired from working overtime all week. As I entered my home gathering the mail, I threw my purse on the buffet table and sat down on the couch. I laid back, and my daughter Tanya began to race through my mind. I asked *God,* "Lord what did she do to deserve this? I need some answers. You took my husband and now the only child I have is out there doing *God* knows what? Take me Lord, take me." I cried, and cried, not understanding why. I wanted her safe, at home with me and her daughter.

But just as loud as I was telling *God* about how I felt, *God* spoke back to me, *"Why not your child? I gave my Son up for you, but just like I returned him back to me, I will return her back to you..."*

Still crying, my heart and soul replied, "Yes Lord, Yes Lord...I'll do whatever you want me to do, I'll say whatever you want me to say, if you lead me, I'll follow, I'll obey. I won't stray, Jesus, and I won't be afraid anymore. Let thy will be done Lord." At that very moment a calm sense of peace came over me.

The next day I returned to work. Tears would flow down my face, confusing my co-workers, who would ask with concern, "What's wrong Shirley?"

I replied, "All is well, all is well."

They didn't know that my tears were not of *sorrow* anymore but they were tears of *joy.* In my heart I knew now that *God* was going to bring her back to me. Even though I didn't know *the day* nor *the hour,* I just knew what I knew. So I turned my daughter over to Jesus...

I also prayed for the other addicts I saw when I was at the crack house that day. My daughter didn't know this but there was a young man at the gas station when I stopped for gas. I was prepared to hit him with my purse when he ap-

proached me, aware of the area I was in—it was very danger-
ous. He saw me when I came for my daughter and said to me,
"Miss, Miss, can you pray for me? I have no one looking for
me."

My heart went out to that young man, and I asked him
right then and there if he believed that Jesus died on the cross
for him and rose that he might have life.

He said, "Yes."

I told him, "Now you're saved." And that's all it took.

I've been told he died in the madness of his addiction,
but at least he was *SAVED*...

*For GOD so loved the world that he gave his one and
only Son, that whoever believes in him shall not perish, but
have eternal life...*

John 3:16

CHAPTER FIFTEEN

"Let me go! Stop, Please stop! I don't know what you're talking about; you're hurting me..."

Kidnapped again; these same kidnappers held my cousin Daryl and another guy for over a week before getting a hold of me. They beat him in his head with a gun, causing him to receive twenty-three stitches. They also took a lighter to his friend and burned his private parts. These sick idiots hung these men by their waists completely naked with their hands tied behind their backs. The kidnappers were two brothers that were getting high themselves and were overly paranoid. They believed someone was after them every time they got high and they claimed Daryl and his friend knew who it was. After that, they hosed them down with water and continued to whip them with black extension cords. Finally, after days of torture, one of the brothers received a call from their oldest brother in Atlanta who knew Daryl, and was told to let them go. Daryl and his friend rushed to stop a cab and went straight to the hospital; that saved their lives.

I was hanging around the "Dead End" at one of the crack houses when the same two kidnappers came to cop. They saw me and immediately asked, "You have a cousin named Daryl right?"

I answered, "Yeah."

"I thought he introduced us to you a while back. You alright? You good?"

"I'm good," I replied.

"Well, would you like to come with us? We're getting ready to party; you and your girl can come along."

Some referred to "getting ready to party" as getting high. We were used to being invited, but there was always a cost, nothing was free. The girl I was with was headed to go smoke with a friend of hers, so I left with them thinking, *"He's a friend of my cousin Daryl; it should be fine."*

On our way to their place we stopped at a convenience store. I walked in, and they told me to get whatever I wanted. I put cigarettes, grape soda, a bag of chips and a toothbrush on the counter. I'd always find some kind of way to clean my teeth whether if it was with toothpaste or Arm and Hammer baking soda—remembering what Mrs. Peaches told me—even if I had to use my finger. I would even take dishwashing liquid when available to wash all my private body parts when I could, but that was far and few in-between.

As we arrived at their house, I noticed each door and window was covered with iron gates. You could see that the house was unkempt, once inside. There was also a foul odor that lingered throughout the house. But all I was really concerned about was getting high—they had purchased plenty.

We proceeded downstairs into the basement where they immediately fixed a pipe with a big solid rock and passed it to me to go first. It was chivalry, drug style. They lit the torch for me as I inhaled smoothly. I passed the rest to them because it was such a large amount. They took turns adding more and more—smoke was everywhere. They passed it back to me and when I lit the pipe and inhaled, while holding the smoke in, I fell to the floor unconscious.

One of them hit me in the head from behind. I'm not sure how long I was actually out, but I do know when I came to, they were still sitting around getting high. I could vaguely see, and the first question out of their mouth was, "Who's looking for us?"

"What you talking about?" I asked.

"B#*&#, you know what we're talking about, when they coming?" He asked while hitting me with a baseball bat in one hand and smoking the pipe in the other.

"Stop, Please Stop, I don't know what you're talking about," I answered, screaming in agony.

His arm then struck me squarely in the face causing my nose to bleed profusely. In addition to my two black eyes, I was sexually abused, strangled and repeatedly asked to stab myself with a knife or they would do it for me—so I did. My body wrenched in pain and exhaustion, as the violence continued over the course of four days. I just knew that my life was about to be over; until they finally fell asleep. I silently prayed to *God, "God* where are you? I trusted you to be here to comfort me, to lessen the pain when it became unbearable and to give me the strength when I felt weak and powerless, where are you?"

But I will restore you to health and heal your wounds declares the Lord, because you are called an outcast, from whom no one cares...

Jeremiah 30:17

When I attempted to proceed towards the stairs, one of them woke up. He looked at me in a type of exhausted disgust and said, "Where you think you going?"

"I need to use the bathroom," I replied.

"Bring your ass right back," he said.

"OK," I answered calmly.

All I could think of; how was I going to escape. The house was gated and locked up tighter than Fort Knox. I scurried upstairs to the bathroom, locking the door behind me.

The bathroom had the only window that was without bars, but it was on the second level of the house making escape even more difficult. When I raised the window to glance out quickly, I saw a very lengthy drop. I had to jump. I had no other choice, I couldn't take any more torture—eventually they would kill me. So I climbed out, positioning myself for a hang jump, in hopes that the fall wouldn't kill me either...It was the lesser of the two evils.

Hanging there from the window helpless and still shivering in fear, I whispered to myself, *"I'll be okay,"* convincing myself that I could make the jump. But knowing they would soon wake up and start abusing me all over again gave me the courage to immediately let go.

When I hit the ground my reaction to the pain was quick, bouncing me back into reality. I quickly tried to run for my life; I wasn't naked this time, but I surely wasn't in the best shape with fresh stab wounds, a bloody nose and lip, all the bruises...and the fall. I was in serious pain.

"Please answer, please!"

The door opened to the neighbor's house. "Oh *God*! What happened to you?" the neighbor asked.

"I was held hostage by your neighbors next door and I escaped out of the second level bathroom window."

The neighbor immediately let me in and called the police, as I continued to explain, "They're still in the house asleep, they're high on crack and they have guns!"

When the police arrived they asked me a ton of questions. They had me describe the two guys in detail, while another car was called to go to their house.

I watched the police bring the guys out in handcuffs and put them in the back of the squad car; I felt such a relief come over me. The police thought I should go to the hospital to get checked out, but I insisted that with a little ice and ointment I would be fine. I couldn't take the chance of being arrested for violating my probation again. One of the cops handed me a business card, instructing me to call the detective bureau and follow-up Thursday with the kidnapping and rape division; then they left.

I had the best intentions to see this through, to have these guys put behind bars for what they had done to me. Yet, even after all that, *I still* wanted to get high.

CHAPTER SIXTEEN

A ll the pain, despair and abuse had now become a way of life for me. I had accepted all this as my destiny. The following Thursday, the guys were released from jail because I never reported to the detective like I was instructed to do. I was back at square one—"The Dead End..."

Within weeks of this incident it seemed I was in an emotional wasteland, worse than ever—worse than any other time. I finally hit rock bottom, at least my bottom. I became very tired, overly discouraged and paranoid of everything. My own self-respect as well as any respect anybody else had left for me was completely gone...finally the only solution for me was death. But first... *"I'll take one last trip to the crack house, and then I'll end my Life."*

"What? Know ye not that your body is the temple of the Holy Ghost which is in you, which ye have of God, and ye are not your own? For ye are bought with a price: therefore glorify God in your body, and in your spirit, which are God's"

1Corinthians 6:19-20

He upholds the cause of the oppressed and gives food to the hungry. The Lord sets prisoners free; The Lord gives sight to the blind, The Lord lifts up those who are bowed down, The Lord loves the righteous. The Lord watches over the alien and sustains the fatherless and the widow, but he frustrates the ways of the wicked...

Psalm 147:7-9

"Don't panic," I whispered. "They'll go away," Trying to tell the others.

No one was paying me any attention, everyone was still getting high and I was frantic. I slowly crawled towards the window and peeked out. I was confused as to why my mother was there with the police. Was she here to turn me in? Why would she do this to me? So many things streamed through my mind all at once. Like bolts of lighting, it flashed back—the rape, the kidnapping, the abuse, the fire, and what would come next if I didn't stop getting high.

Soon the knocking became a relentless pounding that shook the door frame. I wanted to escape out the back door, through the vacant lot behind the house and keep running until I found another place to smoke. But I was out of resources and I was really sick and tired of it all.

The door finally ripped clean off the hinges, and the police ran in to arrest us. "There she is officer," I heard my mother say. I despised my mother at that very moment, thinking, *"Why would she bring them here?"*

The trip to the police station was the culmination of nearly nine years of helplessness and struggle. I was hesitant to believe I had any chance of successfully getting unhooked from this drug on my own. My confidence to follow through was stripped away. Of course my attempt to stay clean was obviously what I needed. But I wouldn't dare mention this to anyone. I would have been met with disbelief. After all, I had tried this more than once, so keeping my thoughts of wanting to be clean and sober to myself just made sense to me.

After returning to the cold cement cell and a cot once again, I realized that this time I'd probably be doing some serious time. It was my second time violating my probation. I was feeling doomed, lying there without my pipe in my hand and no crack to smoke. It only left me with thoughts of why I didn't just wait there for the kidnappers to kill me, which might have been easier.

I couldn't imagine what was next for me. I did not have no hopes, no dreams, nor did I have my daughter, my family or man to go home to anymore. My own mother turned me in. So what was next?

"Lord is this it? Is this what you had planned for my life, Alpha and Omega...I have no one and nothing now. I'm at my bottom and I'm tired, this can't be the ending. I'd rather die. I'm crying out to you Lord, I need your help to make my life right. I'm realizing I can't do it by myself."

Do not hold against me the sins of the fathers, may your mercy come quickly to meet me for I am in desperate need...

Psalm 79:8

Then they cried to the Lord in their trouble, and he saved them from their distress. He brought them out of darkness and the deepest gloom and broke away their chains...

Psalm 107:13-14

As the tears streamed down my face, I knew that I would need to face my addiction, my many sorrows, and all my trials and tribulations. This intense difficulty of my circumstances culminated with sickness and exhaustion. It took all of that, for me to realize that **I Needed Help.**

CHAPTER SEVENTEEN

T he next day, before the judge, several of us were being sentenced. Hearing the sentencing of others that went before me let me know it wasn't looking good. Some were being sentenced to life without parole, others five years or more. I had only done six months or less in jail before. The one thing that could save me was that my file clearly documented my drug problem—that would make it impossible for the courts not to know that my crimes with checks and credit card fraud and the theft were to support my addiction. Maybe the possibility of being sent to Rehab would enter the judge's mind.

The court-appointed attorney told me to follow him; we entered into a room in the back of the judge's chambers. He sat me down to discuss the deal he had made and explained that I should consider the plea. The prosecutor was offering me 24-60 months. I couldn't seem to comprehend the months into years quick enough, "How many years is that because this sounds like it's a lot?"

"It could be two years minimum or up to five years maximum," he responded.

"Oh my *God!*" All I heard was five years. "I can't do five years!"

"You'll be in a camp, you can do it," he replied.

"Camp, County! I can't do this."

Not that I couldn't do it, I didn't want to do it. "Why

can't they just put me in Rehab, that's what you said might happen."

"You have too many violations for not showing up Tanya, I have nothing else to bargain with, nothing." He replied.

Of course, after I heard that, I really wanted to leave and go get high, so it was probably best.

The judge sentenced me to two years with parole. I left the courtroom without saying good-bye to anyone, not even my mother who was right there staring me straight in my face. I didn't look in her direction. All I kept thinking was she caused all this to happen.

As an addict, you blame everyone but yourself, even to have a reason to use. And it could be any reason: the dog died, it's too hot, too cold, whatever! Something as simple as that...

As I sat in the county jail waiting for the feds to pick me up, I was becoming increasingly angry and bitter with every passing moment. Not to mention the withdrawals I was going through of wanting another hit. Finally, when I returned to my cell, I fell asleep for what seemed like two complete months. I remembered how long ago it had been since I had a good night's sleep; oh yeah, when my grandfather and I would sit at the dock of the bay watching the waves and the seagulls. Now the only time I would wake up was when my food was brought to me and to use the bathroom. Even then, most times I'd just roll over instead of eating, because the food was that terrible.

As I heard my name being called my stomach began boiling over. I wasn't ready to do my time, but I was ready to leave where I was. I was headed to Ft. Worth, Texas to a co-ed Federal Prison Camp; a prison where most celebrities and white collar crime offenders were sent to do their sentence.

I boarded a government air craft and I assure you, it wasn't as glamorous as the plane ride to Los Angeles, California to see my friend Kim. I was handcuffed and shackled around my stomach area and my ankles with five other inmates. The airplane was filled with other criminals chained the same way. I headed towards the back of the plane, passing all these men who were acting like vultures, winking and sticking their tongues out in a disgusting way.

When we arrived at the Federal Prison Camp, after being handcuffed and shackled for hours, it was a relief to have them removed. I was taken to R&D (receiving and discharge) where I went through a host of events: finger printing, mug shots, I.D., clothing, etc. Then they proceeded to bring a group of us a meal while we waited for an officer to escort us to our housing unit.

While walking up the hill, I noticed that the inmates were dressed in their own clothing, and the men and women were congregating together. I knew I was coming to a co-ed facility but what I didn't know was that we shared everything: eating, activities, classes, the work place, church and recreation, everything except sleeping quarters.

My living quarters was a far cry from the crack houses I was living in. There was a twin bed with a real mattress, a closet, a desk, and there was also central heating and air. When I walked past the mirror hanging on one of the walls and saw how I looked, that's when I realized just how horrible of a sight I really was. My hair was still short, my face had multiple scars and I had two stab wounds located on my right thigh. My self-esteem was the lowest it had ever been, and on top of all that—the anger, bitterness, and resentment I felt was overwhelming.

Now we see but a poor reflection in the mirror, then we shall see face to face. Now I know in part, then I shall know fully, even as I am fully known...

1 Corinthians 13:12

My roommate walked in and immediately welcomed me; her name was Melody. She would be my "Bunkie" as it's referred to in prison. She was a beautiful light skinned black woman and about the same age as I, if not a tad bit older. She was also from Detroit. Melody was the background singer for the singing group, "Parliament Funkadelics" with lead singer George Clinton. She went on to remind me of their hit songs, "One Nation Under a Groove" and "Atomic Dog". The classic part of the lyrics she sung, "Why must I feel like that, why must I chase the cat," and the group would reply, "Nothing but the dog in me."

I told her, "I remember that, wow!"

Melody had a beautiful voice. We became friends fast and would talk for hours at a time. Every night before bed I would talk her into singing something, anything just so I could fall asleep. Melody didn't consider herself an addict at all, but she was definitely one you would call a *Functional Addict.*" She consumed large amounts of cocaine while touring on the road. But we had one major thing in common—we both were there to try and kick our habits.

As the weeks passed, I began to take interest in my appearance and personal hygiene. Melody and some of the others who had been there for a while had given me some toiletries, clothing and extra things they had to help me out. I began to fix my hair, remembering some of the ways I used to wear it. My first attempt must have been pretty good because I received many compliments about how my hair looked. Those compliments back then were worth millions; they gave me a sense of pride I hadn't had for many years.

The women were nice and I began to bond with them. We carefully listened to each other and what we had all been through, one story sadder than the next. But there was one thing we all related to—**ABUSE**. We had been used, wounded, broken and we had hurt others, but through this, we all found *God*. We began to help one another walk through this process, and one of my contributions was making sure the hair was right.

I began attending the church services on the camp grounds. The Preachers and Evangelists from the outside world would come in on the weekends and bring us the word of the Lord. As I loosened up and started to heal from my adversity, I joined the usher board and the dance teams, using gifts I didn't even know I had. I started to read, hear, and live the word for myself and attend N.A. (Narcotics Anonymous) meetings. I humbled myself and did some serious soul searching. When I did this, a spirit of reconciliation became a great part of my journey back. I openly examined and confessed my faults not just to myself, but to *God* and to others who I trusted. I evaluated all my relationships, offering forgiveness to those who had hurt me and made amends for the harm I had caused to others. After doing all this, I finally understood what my mother had done was definitely for my own good. I wrote her a letter thanking her for loving me enough to not only have me arrested but for never giving up on me, never...

> *Dear Mother,*
>
> *I now know why you did what you did that day. I can only thank you from the bottom of my heart. To know that I have a mother that will do whatever it takes, by any means necessary to keep me safe from harm and danger. You have given me a chance to get myself together even if it took for me to be arrested and jailed. I thank you for that. I'm really doing well Mom, and I know you, Granddaddy and Grandma would be proud. I won't say much more. Just know that God is working it all out. Tell everyone I love them and give Parisia a big hug and kiss for me.*
>
> *Love, Your Daughter*

I didn't go into all the details at that time. I just wanted her to know that I understood her motive and I finally got it.

Brother I do not consider myself yet to have taken hold of it. But one thing I do; forgetting what is behind and reaching toward what is ahead. I press on towards the goal to win the prize for which God has called me heavenward in Christ Jesus...

Philippians 3:13-14

Seeds of shame were sown and fertilized throughout my addiction. But one day at a time I began to tell myself, that was yesterday and this is today. I recognize now that my life is full of meaning and full of discovery. I no longer rush to a halfhearted conclusion or a quick fix. I just need to take my time and accept life on life's terms. Better yet, I told myself, know that **this too shall pass**...

CHAPTER EIGHTEEN

A fter much playing around with different hair styles and such, the other inmates thought I was good at what I did, and they all started requesting me to do their hair. I was using some of them as "guinea pigs," trying out new styles that I saw on television shows, having everyone look trendy and up to date. We had most of the hair essentials and tools we needed, but we weren't allowed to have scissors in our units. Scissors back then were considered contraband. Scissors could only be used in the Cosmetology program and the waiting list was a mile long. My chances of getting into that program were slim to none considering the length of sentence I had, and I was not trying to stay any longer.

Back then, in the mid-'80s, the haircut everyone was wearing was called the "Asymmetrical," where one side of the hair was shorter that the other. One day I was lying in my bed and I glanced over at the toenail clipper that was lying on my locker. I immediately thought, *"I wonder if I can cut my hair with those."* I hopped up from my bed and stood in the mirror, taking small amounts of hair and clipping each section until I created a Chinese bang that was cut evenly straight across. I couldn't wait until the next day to try this technique on the other inmates.

There were so many haircuts that I had done walking around the compound that weren't done in Cosmetology that the unit guard commenced a lock down in search of scissors. It took the one guard who would listen to my explanation of how these cuts were being done with a toenail clipper. After the guard saw how I accomplished these cuts, even she was impressed. "If you can do this with a toenail clipper what will you do when they put a pair of scissors in your hand? We'll probably see you on the cover of a magazine with this big toenail clipper in your hand." Funny…she was actually speaking about something that would be in my future.

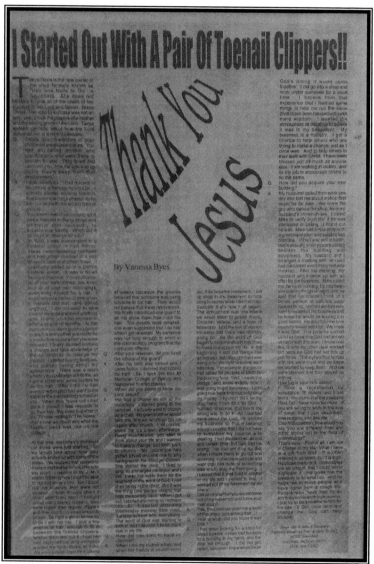

My story was later reported in the newspaper

Later that week my granddaddy came to visit me. He was so proud to see me with the weight I had put on, refreshed, and a smile on my face again. It had been such a long time since anyone saw me healthy, including myself. We were having such a great time at our visit, with me sharing everything I had been doing with him. I also mentioned the job I had acquired as an ADT operator with one of the contracts through UNICOR, where we placed mail through a machine that sorted the mail by zip code (and you might not know this but some inmates were actually your 411 operators too). It made sense that a company would rather pay inmates four-hundred dollars a month than pay four-hundred a week plus benefits to their own employees. But I had a job, and Granddaddy was very happy and proud.

I think at that moment, he even knew what my mother had done was best for me. All the turmoil I had put him through, all appeared to be erased with one visit. I could see his big, big grin as I waved good-bye to him. I knew my granddaddy was going back to brag about the great things he heard and saw for himself.

Three weeks later, my granddaddy passed away. It was very disturbing since it was Grandmother who was ill. Granddaddy had a clean bill of health. When I received the news, I swear the whole compound heard my screams of agony. I couldn't seem to get myself together. They had to sedate me just to calm me down. When I finally woke up, I prayed that it was just a dream.

I asked Melody, "Tell me I was dreaming and my granddaddy's not dead." She replied, "I'm so sorry honey, but it's true." She grabbed me and rocked me in her arms as if I was her little girl.

The next day I reported to the chapel with Melody right by my side. I made all the arrangements and she and the choir planned what we call a "Home Going" (a celebration of Life) in remembrance of my granddaddy. At the Home Going

I received so many sympathy cards that I couldn't read them all. The cards were from inmates I had never met around the compound; I thought it was very considerate of them. The choir sung till Heaven got the news and the eulogy was done so beautifully by the Chaplin. The Chaplin and I had had many conversations, some even included my granddaddy. She knew exactly how much I loved him and what he meant to me.

Later I met with my counselor who prepared documents for a furlough (a temporary release), so I could be approved to go home for the services. I received a five day unescorted furlough. I had already determined in my mind that if I had to be shackled, I wouldn't attend. Once again *God* spared me with his grace and mercy.

When it came time for me to leave for Detroit, I was not only prepared to see my granddaddy put to rest, but excited about seeing my daughter Parisia too. She was now four years old. I had already missed her first words, her first birthday, even her first steps.

"Will she know who I am? Will she even come to me?" I asked myself.

Whatever I was facing, I knew I needed to focus on something just as important—NOT USING. For an addict the real challenge is when you face the outside world and still stay clean. Rehab and Prison have this sort of wall of protection around you. First of all, you don't have the drugs, the people, the places or the things that are part of the madness. It's easy when things are not available to you. But now I was challenged with this life or death responsibility, which I had always failed to do in the past—leave prison on my own and be trusted to return back in five days like instructed, all while staying clean.

I had worked very hard to receive the level of community custody, and everything around me felt good now. I could look in the mirror at myself and be pleased at what I saw. My hair had grown out and was healthy, my skin had cleared up and my teeth were in great shape (*thanks to Miss Peaches' homespun wisdom of Arm & Hammer Baking Soda*). I was physically fit from exercising and I wore a smile on my face again. I was in good spirits even through my time of bereavement. My granddaddy last saw me clean and sober and he was proud of me, and that made all the difference for me to accept his death.

When I arrived home, my mother was there to pick me up. We hugged and kissed and she said, "Look at you, you look beautiful."

"Thank you Mom."

That was a far stretch from how terrible I had looked the last time she had seen me. We got in the car and went straight to the mall. She wanted me to find something off-white to wear for the services. The norm for a funeral was to wear black, but that seemed to have changed, and it wasn't as much mourning, as it was celebrating life. I was grateful I had my time to grieve out of the way; I knew my family was still prepared for me to fall over in the casket with grief. But what they didn't realize, I had grown in the word of *God* while I was away. It might have been different if he had died when I was in my madness. I would have been torn to pieces knowing smoking crack would have taken precedence over the burial of my granddaddy like it had for Jessie. *"God knows how much we can bear."*

While shopping at the mall I ran into a couple of people I went to high school with. Everyone knew I had been strung out on crack—it wasn't any secret—and they were no exception. They expressed their condolences, never mentioning anything about my addiction. Yet I knew eventually I had to face the ridicule and judgment of others, which was one of my greatest fears to overcome. But I was definitely going to work on it.

We arrived at my grandparents' house and Parisia was upstairs playing in one of the bedrooms. As I approached the first landing, I looked up toward the next flight of stairs and there she was, just as pretty as I imagined she would be. She had really thick ponytails with all these bows in her hair, and a smile that lit up the room. When I approached the top of the stairs, I picked her up and she gave me the biggest hug, until she saw my mother. She immediately reached out for her. I didn't make things complicated; I just accepted whatever she was willing to give me. I knew the harm I had caused and I was ready to accept full responsibility for my own actions. That day I learned a great deal about my baby just by watching her play and how she interacted with others. It let me know my mother and Paris had done such a great job raising her.

I walked into the bedroom where I had spent a lot of quality time with my granddaddy. Grandmother was sitting in her usual chair. I walked over to her without saying a word and just sat in her lap like I was five years old again, laying my head on her shoulder. My granddaddy was her whole life, outside of the church. I sat quietly, reminiscing with nothing but joy in my heart, while Grandmother rubbed my head letting me know everything was going to be alright.

The funeral was packed with family and friends. People came from all over to pay their respects: Ohio, St. Louis, Mississippi, and Texas. Most of them had known who I was but I couldn't quite remember them. Was this one of the side effects from the drug—lack of memory? As I sat there on the front row while people were still walking by Granddaddy, someone gently grabbed my hand and said, "Tanya, you ok?" I looked up; it was Paris. He was just as attractive as he had always been, dressed in all black with a clergy collar. I didn't know he was there to deliver the Eulogy, but it made sense; he knew Granddaddy so well.

It was nice to see him in action in his ministry, and boy could he preach! He was a natural and you could tell that the calling on his life was real. We didn't get a chance to say much afterwards; he had his lady friend with him and he seemed happy, really happy. I only wanted the best for him. I had done enough damage to this man, and besides he was still Parisia's father; nothing could change that. I had hoped we would always remain friends, but for right now, I just needed to stay focused and concentrate on **ME!**

After we left the repast I returned to my grandparents' house; I was exhausted. I went straight into my granddaddy's room and Parisia and I fell asleep. She didn't sleep long; she woke up crying looking for my mother. Once she saw her, the crying stopped. She looked at me confused, probably wondering, "Who is this lady?" I didn't press the issue or go into any details of who I was because I knew I would be leaving her again to return back to prison.

The next day, many of my friends that attended the funeral decided to stop by the house to see me. They wanted to take me out to dinner and clubbing, which I believed was all so innocent, of course. But what they didn't understand was that my life had completely changed. In order for me to stay clean and sober, I could no longer do the things I used to do. Plus, I would be risking a violation. I was still under Bureau of Prison (B.O.P.) custody. I realized my mission in Detroit was finished. Granddaddy was laid to rest, I had spent time with my family, I saw my beautiful daughter and I wanted to remain the way I came—**CLEAN and SOBER**...

I made a decision to return back to prison camp early. Finally, I could see the bigger picture. I didn't think anything was wrong with this decision, but trying to tell my mother was a different story.

"Baby, why are you leaving so early? You don't have to be back for two more days," she said.

But what she failed to realize, I was still fighting temptation. My recovery was still in early stages. Most of my family and friends were drinking, smoking weed and ready to paint the town red, and even though none of this was my real drug of choice *I still* wasn't ready or able to be around this kind of behavior...***People, Places, or Things***.

People and family in general don't realize that an addict can't be around those sorts of things—not even the lifestyle that comes along with it—especially in recovery. Some addicts think they can, but we can't. I guess my friends felt like it wasn't crack, so I should be fine. An addict can't be around any drugs or alcohol, or most prescription drugs...A drug...is a drug...is a drug.

I left the next day on the first flight headed to Texas. I remember returning to prison and being asked many questions by the officer "Aren't you supposed to return on Friday? It's Wednesday."

"I know sir; I wanted to make sure I was here on time."

"Never seen this happen before," he replied.

I wanted to tell him; *"Maybe they didn't have an addiction they were struggling with; I'm trying my best to stay clean,"* but I kept it to myself.

After knowing my granddaddy was at peace, seeing Parisia and watching my family smile at me again, it gave me the motivation and ambition to continue to move forward; besides, my family needed me. Now my Mother was faced to take care of her mother with an illness and Parisia by herself. Mother would always set aside her own life for others. She sold her house and moved in with Grandmother, because Grandmother didn't want to leave her home, even though her neighborhood had gotten worse. My mother was back on "The Ocean".

CHAPTER NINETEEN

For some reason, prison had become a safe haven for me. If there was anything illegal going on, for the first time I didn't know about it and for once I didn't care to search for it either. I was feeling content, enjoying my life being clean. In my spare time I learned how to play tennis, and racquetball, I took long walks and read many books. I even joined the cheerleading team and played softball. I explored many crafts like pottery, one-stroke painting and card making, things I probably would have never done even if I wasn't using crack. I was attending N. A. meetings regularly learning all about "The Twelve Steps".

A few months later, my counselor told me that I was being considered for a parole hearing, as long as I kept progressing, programming and staying out of trouble—incident free. It appeared that freedom would be coming sooner than later…

I continued to do what was expected of me and it was now time to appear before the parole board. There were two decisions that could be made: the first was, to be reduced to nine months from my original two year sentence. The second was, I could be denied.

When I entered the room and sat down, I can't tell you how fast my heart was beating, and trying to keep from perspiring. They asked many questions about my addiction, ultimately to determine if I thought I was ready to enter back into society with narcotics being available to me.

My answer was, "All I can do is try, take one day at a

time, but I will continue my meetings regularly."

They continued to ask other questions like, where would I live, with whom, and what were my goals. I now had three goals: continue to fight this disease, build a relationship with my daughter and enroll into Cosmetology School to get my license. I was told to step into the hallway and wait for someone to call me back into the room.

While waiting I asked *God*, *"Please God, I know I've asked you for so many things before, but if you could just this one time please be on my side, I would be so grateful."* I was nervous, feeling non-deserving of anything I asked *God* for. I mean why would *God* grant me anything? All the promises I made to him and hadn't kept any of them; I was at his mercy…

I was told to come inside and have a seat. One of the parole board members began to speak, "Tanya Harp 06460-039, we have made our decision and we have concluded that your sentence will be reduced to nine months, and you will be paroled in two months. You will report to your assigned parole officer within seventy-two hours after your release date and you will continue to report as instructed for the remaining time left on your sentence, which is fifteen months. Also you will continue to make N.A. meetings at least three times a week; there will be a weekly form where you will have the representative sign every time you attend. We are giving you this chance based on your behavior and the programming you have done here at Fort Worth. Now you're not off the hook just yet, so continue to do what you've been doing for the remainder of your time left here. Any incidents will violate the agreement and cancel any decision we have made here today. Good Luck! And we hope we never see you again."

"Thank You! Thank You! I'm going to do my best," I replied.

I left looking for Melody and the others, to give them

the good news. When I saw the girls, they were ready to cele-
brate right along with me. I was the last of my group to receive a release date.

*But many that are first shall be last; and the last shall be
first...*

Matthew 19:30

During my last two months I worked out hard, getting
my body tight and in shape. I hadn't done any dating, but I
did have a male friend named Vincent from Washington, DC
who I enjoyed playing tennis and racquetball with from time
to time. I kept myself very busy between doing hair, taking
classes, work, N.A. meetings, church and recreation; the time
flew by.

Finally, it was time to say good-bye. I was going to
miss so many from my circle of prison friends. They had been
a very positive force, even the tough love they had given me,
it was all so needed. That morning when I was getting ready
to leave, fear seemed to tap me on the shoulder. All these
questions began to stir up in my head as I was packing: *"Are
you really going to stay clean?" "You can do just one before
going to the house."*

Where were these thoughts coming from? I thought
they were gone. Why was this all resurfacing once again? I
began to scream, "NO! NO! NO!"

Melody walked in. "Tanya! What's wrong?" She
asked.

"I don't know...all these thoughts of using again...
where is this coming from? I'm scared," I replied.

Right then she grabbed my hand and began to pray...

"Father God, you know everything about us, you are

the beginning and the end, the Alpha and Omega, I ask you right now to order her steps. We have not come this far to allow the adversary to take control; we ask that you bind him completely—he will not come today to kill, steal or destroy her in Jesus name. We ask that you cover her with your blood and send your grace and have mercy as she makes this transition back into society. You have equipped her with an anointed gift to use to become successful. I ask that she continue to seek you first, the kingdom of GOD and we know everything will be added unto her in Jesus name. So right now we ask for traveling mercy as she travels to her final destination, and that's with her family and her beautiful daughter. All these things we ask of you Jesus, Amen!"

"Now Tanya, you know what to do and what not to do. Let's do this, you can do it girl! *God* has blessed you with early release and he makes no mistakes, none. I love you and I wish you the best. Just do exactly what you did here and I know you'll be alright; I'm four months behind you, okay!"

"Okay," I replied.

We hugged, and it was time to leave. I left the unit walking to R & D to be discharged. Everyone was showering me with well wishes: "Don't want to see you back here!" "Good Luck and be good!" "I'm going to look you up to do my hair, girl!" "Be Blessed!"

They all knew I could do it; I just needed to know I could. Right when the van pulled up to take me to the airport, I knew it was time to stand and stand strong and tall.

When I boarded the airplane and took my seat, I heard my granddaddy say, *"You did it."* I could see that big grin he would always have on his face. While flying in the air, I wondered what my crazy friends were doing; we had such good times together in spite of our situation. I also prayed that they would soon see these beautiful clouds I was now seeing. I knew I would always remember them; they were a part of my journey, and a part of my recovery. I thank *God* for placing them in my life even if it meant I had to come to prison to meet them.

   While walking to baggage claim, the anticipation of being back in society and seeing all the people let me know how real it was that I was out of prison; my life was about to change. I had many things that I would be challenged with in hopes that I would be making all the right decisions. Mother was there to pick me up with Parisia sleeping in the back seat. I crawled back there anyway, just to look at her as a reminder of why I needed to stay focused. I didn't jump into anything fast at first. I just enjoyed the long talks with Mother and Grandmother and holding Parisia, getting acquainted with her. Even though rejection still took place, I was willing to work on step one: ***Accept the things I cannot change...***

CHAPTER TWENTY

I was now excited about going to church; for me, the word of *God* was the greatest force of strength. Hearing the word of *God* was how I survived every week, along with hearing other addicts share their stories around the tables at my meetings; it brought me such great comfort.

When I was preparing for church that Sunday morning, I was a little nervous. In my mind I imagined that church on the outside always appeared to be filled with perfect people, and I was thinking I simply wouldn't fit in. I mean let's face it, I'm definitely not perfect. When I attended church in prison, I had known we all had fallen short and sinned, and that made me feel as though I belonged.

When we drove up to Mt. Sinai Baptist Church where my family presently attended, we had to park across the street. As we were walking towards the church, I noticed that the area looked very familiar to me. I looked for the gas station that used to be on the corner; it had closed down, but you could still tell that it used to be there. I told my mother to wait a minute, while I ran to the corner to see if the building I used to get high in was still there, and it was. It was abandoned, with all the windows and doors boarded up. This was the building I was coming out of and the gas station where Paris was parked when he came to talk to me years back. Then suddenly, I realized the church I was about to walk into actually was the same church where I used to sit on the steps high.

I reminded my mother about the area and we were both blown away. Mother mentioned her church had just moved into this building temporarily six months ago, and it never dawned on her that this was the same area.

I entered into Sunday school and one of the ministers was teaching a powerful message. It set up conviction in my heart and I was lead to join immediately. The classroom was small and intimate, and the process of becoming a member was very simple. After class was over, I met back up with my family and shared what I had done; they were both elated.

When morning service started the sanctuary was packed. I thought to myself, *"I'm glad I joined in Sunday school because I might have been afraid to take that long walk all the way to the front of the church, in front of all these people."* But what I didn't know was that the Pastor had everyone who joined in Sunday school stand up and share their name with the whole congregation. I listened to the others acknowledge their presence. Most would say their name, and their type of membership; if they had family members or friends in the congregation, they would acknowledge them too.

Then it was my turn, "My name is Tanya Harp, my mother is Shirley Harp..."

Before I could finish, they began to clap and shout "Amen" and "Hallelujah", because they knew who I was; they had all been praying for me.

I continued, "I'm here to be baptized..."

They started up again. I was a taken off guard by their actions, but it did make me feel welcome. After the service, my family and I went to dinner and discussed how excited and proud they were. I shared how coincidental it was, that the church I joined was the same church steps I sat on many nights.

For I know the plans I have for you," declares the Lord, "Plans to prosper you and not to harm you, plans to give you hope and a future. Then you will call upon me, and come and pray to me, and I will listen to you. You will seek me and find me, when you seek me with all your heart. I will be found by you," declares the Lord, "And I will bring you back from captivity. I will gather you from all nations, places where I have banished you," declares the Lord, "And bring you back to the place from which I carried you into exile...

Jeremiah 29:11-14

That week I found several N.A. meetings in my area to attend. One person at the meeting told me to make as many meetings as I could, reasoning, "As addicts, we didn't go to just one crack house; we went to several in one day, not just all day but all night—with no excuses."

I noticed that there were many different kinds of addicts: some were there because it was mandatory, some were addicts who were seeking relationships and sexual partners, some were addicts that were still active in using while making meetings, and some were addicts who thought they could go back to selling drugs as a means of income (these types of addicts are the kind that would eventually start using again), but there were also the type of addicts that really wanted to receive help. You just had to make a decision—**Why are we Here?**

Let us not give up meeting together, as some are in the habit of doing, but let us encourage one another—and all the more as you see the Day approaching...

Hebrews 10:25

When I attended the N.A. meetings, I just listened to the others share their stories and advice. We have a saying: If you haven't done the things you hear others say they did in their addiction, put a "yet" on it; meaning, you haven't done it *yet*, but keep using, and eventually you will.

Life was unfolding beautifully. My relationship with my daughter was mending nicely together; Parisia was even calling me Momma. It was now time for me to meet the Pastor, Reverend Rufus C. Pope, and I was very nervous about it. What exactly was I going to say to him? Was I going to lie or dance around the truth? I didn't think people in church had done anything wrong, ever. We used to call church folks "goody-two-shoes."

There were two people ahead of me while I was waiting and even they looked like they had been in church all their life—the perfect Christian type. It was my turn; Reverend Pope called my name and told me to have a seat. My hands began to sweat. I kept rubbing them together while he spoke first, "Tanya right."

"Yes sir," I replied.

"Well first I want to say to you, everyone has skeletons in their closet—even me. I used to be an alcoholic."

My eyes turned towards him showing a look of shock; he was talking my language! He continued, "And *God* delivered me, so don't think there aren't any people like you here in church. The church is a hospital for all the wounded."

Wow! That was an eye opener for me, and it gave me the courage to have a conversation with him, one that would be open, honest and way more comfortable than I had anticipated.

I shared how I sat on the church steps many nights, and how I would get high in the building right behind the church and throughout the area. I told him about the time Paris and my mother came for me and the pain I had caused my family, leaving Parisia, and how it all came to an end by me going to prison.

He told me, "Tanya I'm excited about your future. *God* has something awesome planned for your life, and you have a strong testimony, and one day you will stand and share your story with the world."

I thought Rev. Pope had lost his mind. It took all I had to share my story with him; I wasn't about to tell anyone else all this—so I thought.

That Sunday the church was having "Affirmation of faith". This is when Christians get up and tell how *God* has done amazing miracles and deliverance in their lives. This practice was performed to help inspire others by hearing stories that out of darkness, there is always light.

They overcame him by the blood of the lamb and by the words of their testimony...

Revelation 12:11

I stood up two Sundays later to tell my testimony. I shared my story: how I used to sit on the church steps high, how *God* used my mother to have me arrested and sent to prison to help me, how I thought what she did was so horrible and I felt betrayed; but what Satan meant for evil, *God* turned into good.

I didn't really know what to expect, but so many people approached me afterwards to tell me my testimony was a blessing to them. Some even confirmed that, "He's no shorter than his word." Others said, "He's truly an awesome God", "He's a keeper and a healer". Many others told me they would continue to keep me in prayer because I had exposed Satan, and because he'd been defeated, I would probably be under attack.

During his sermon, Rev. Pope suggested to the congregation that we should all get a prayer partner. By this time I had met a few people in the congregation, and Sharon Butler was one of them. She was the daughter of Mother Butler, one our "mothers of the church". Sharon knew a lot about the word of the Lord, and I was very pleased when she approached me to become her partner.

We discussed an appropriate time that we would be

able to call one another daily and decided six o'clock in the evening would be our time of prayer. Most times she would start off leading the prayer. We would pray for the first 15-20 minutes and the other 10-15 minutes we would just talk. I really enjoyed our time on the phone. We talked about every-thing: my recovery, family, friends, and church. Eventually Sharon and I became fond of each other and I even started doing her hair. We were sisters in Christ.

I started seeking out information about what cosmetol-ogy school I would attend. I located two schools in the area: Preston and Anna's School of Beauty and Michigan College of Beauty.

While I was waiting for the bus to go check out the two schools, I ran into Dray. I didn't recognize him at all, but he recognized me. He first mentioned to me how good I looked and asked what I had been up to these past years. I shared that I had been incarcerated and was now in church, attending N.A. meetings and coming up on my one year clean anniversary.

He went on to share that he stopped smoking crack "for a minute", but went back to using occasionally—actually he was on his way home to get high. I told him I didn't care to indulge and was on my way to take care of some important business. He asked for my number to keep in touch and I told him I didn't have one, so he handed me his instead and left. I was really proud of myself—my first tempting moment to use and I stood strong.

After I arrived at the first location, Preston and Anna's, I went inside to find out when the next class was starting and the cost. Back then, the cost was about five thou-sand dollars, and they offered grants, but the class had already started and the next class wasn't starting for another eight months.

I was so determined to become a cosmetologist, I left heading straight across town to Michigan College of Beauty. I sat with the administrator as she confirmed that a class would be starting the following month. She also mentioned that she could go ahead and get started on the paperwork to qualify me for a grant, if I was interested. I was so excited, I hung around for a while checking out the other students, visualizing myself in their shoes soon. Some of the students were really good and already doing professional hair styling. The administrator also mentioned a competition that took place every year. I was already picturing myself as the winner. With everything I viewed that day at the school, I wanted nothing but to start immediately. I left the school with such inspiration and enthusiasm; I couldn't think of anything more exciting than to start working towards my future.

On my way back home, waiting for my bus, I started going through all the information I had gathered from both schools. While looking down, I noticed right beside the bench on the ground someone had left or dropped a broken stem, stuffed with a piece of steel brillo-pad; this kind of object was what we called a poor man's pipe. Seeing this item brought back some memories, making me sense the taste of what it was like. I knew I was being tested. I didn't ponder on it long; I just went back to reading the information. With all these adversities I faced in one day, I felt like *God* was there watching over me. I passed the test with flying colors; I was clearly on my way towards a brighter future.

I returned back to the house. Instantaneously, I shared all the excitement with my family and I even shared my excitement with Sharon during our six o'clock prayer call. What I didn't share with either of them, was that I saw Dray, or the homemade crack pipe I had noticed on the ground; nor did I mention the sudden thought of using, or the sense of taste that ran across my mind. I didn't really know why, I just didn't...

Be self-controlled and alert, your enemy the devil prowls around like a roaring lion looking for someone to devour...

1 Peter 5:8

CHAPTER TWENTY-ONE

An important aspect of my recovery was to get in touch with my long suppressed feelings of using. There was an underlying message signaling me, and if I followed through, it could cause me great danger...But the real disillusionment was yet to come.

The next day I woke up remembering I had an appointment to see my parole officer. When I arrived at his office, he began with the basic routine questions: How was I doing? Any progress I'd like to share? Was I still attending my meetings regularly? And so on...

I told him about the cosmetology school I was planning to attend, my church, and the growth of my relationship with my daughter. I also mentioned to him my life seemed to be going really well. He then instructed me to give a urine specimen for drug testing, which happened at every routine visit. The test results were negative and I was told I could go. I left the office in good spirits; the meeting with my P.O. went very well. I had nothing else to do that day, so I headed home.

The bus pulled up quickly and I was trying to find my bus ticket. As I searched through my jacket pockets, I not only found my ticket but I found a piece of paper with a number on it. After I boarded the bus, I sat down, trying to figure out whose number it was. Baffled for a few minutes, I then realized it was Dray's. Right then I should have thrown it away but I folded it up and put it back in my pocket—like I was saving it for a rainy day—forgetting, ignoring and denying the signs. Would my own actions bring on an opportunity to jeopardize my recovery?

I really believe there is something in our personalities that wants to self-destruct and cries for failure. It's almost like you start to feel like you don't deserve to succeed. The illusion that we can continue to use and stop when we feel like it, certainly seals our own death wish. You can definitely start to feel the change coming over you. Denial quickly returns, along with obsession and compulsion. The disease manifests itself and becomes unbearable to control; when you reach a place where your back is against the wall, you're doomed…

That's when I made the call…

"Dray where are you? I need to see you," I whispered.

I jumped in a cab late that night, without thinking, ignoring all the steps of the program. I didn't think about what I was doing; I just acted on emotions.

I arrived there with only one thing on my mind, remembering that precious diamond stone. When I lit the pipe, I gasped. I held my breath, keeping my eyes on the glass bowl filled with smoke. I pulled as hard as I could, trying to return to that first high that once blew my mind years ago, but I couldn't reach it. This made me chase the high the rest of the night and the following day.

I didn't have much cash to begin with, and Dray had exhausted himself too. I had no possessions of any kind, no jewelry to pawn or sell. I hadn't been in recovery that long to recoup anything of value. All I had was me—my body, and when that was suggested, I knew right then I was back to where I had left off a year ago. There was no starting over, nothing had changed. Why did I allow myself to be put in a position to be manipulated again? I felt hatred of myself, I felt resentment, humiliation and that's when I realized I was out of control again. My daughter, family, church, school, parole, it all flashed through my mind like a movie rewinding itself. Here I was again back at a Dead End...I couldn't believe it!

I didn't want to kill myself, I just felt helpless, like a worthless piece of shit. I didn't know what to do; I was so caught up in the terror of losing everything again. Oh *God*! How did I let this happen? If I had not learned anything else, I learned it was my own choice; I was responsible, there were no excuses and no one to blame. I didn't want to call home and hear the disappointment in their voices again. What were Pastor, the church, and more importantly my parole officer going to say? I was headed back to prison. Oh my *God*! How could I give all this up again! For crack! It's insanity to think I could do the same thing and expect something different to happen, remember! I couldn't imagine myself laying down my body again for crack. It all flashed before me: the cruel, profound things said to me, the kidnappings, the rape, and was the fire next?

Right at that very moment something inside me said, call the name Jesus! *"Jesus! Please! Give me strength to endure this. I don't know if you hear me, but I'm begging you to get me out of here."*

Dray asked, "Who you talking to?"

"JESUS!"

Then without hesitation, I ran straight out the door like Forrest Gump. I ran to the nearest phone booth; the phone was out of order. I saw another across the street. I ran and got inside the booth and began to slide down towards the ground with tears streaming down my face. A stranger knocked on the booth, which startled me; he asked if I needed some help. I spoke, crying, "Yes sir, do you have any change? He handed me a couple of quarters. "Thank you."

I raised myself up to dial my mother, with both hands shaking. She answered, but I hung up the phone. I couldn't face her just yet. I called my prayer partner Sharon. When she answered her voice was calm as the waters standing still, "Hello."

"Sharon."

That's all I could get out before she spoke, "Tanya! Where are you? Let me come get you."

Still crying, "Sharon, I'm so sorry, how could I do this to myself again?"

She replied, "Honey, everything will be alright, I just need to know where you are!"

I looked around to see what street I was on. "I'm on Woodward and Herman Street."

"Stay right there, I'm on my way. Tanya! Don't move I know exactly where you are."

It wasn't long before Sharon arrived. When she saw me she jumped out of her car and grabbed me. With both of us crying, she began to pray right away...

"Father God, all knowing, you said that you were going to bring her back to us and we thank you. She knows too much about you, the Holy Spirit dwells in her. I thank you for keeping her safe from harm and danger and we trust that this part of her life is over! Now use her for your mighty kingdom. Satan lose your hands off of her, you can't have her anymore. You're defeated! Lord I thank you in advance for what we know you're capable of doing. Almighty God in Jesus name, in Jesus name..."

She looked at me and asked, "You ok? Are you hungry? You need anything?"

"No thanks. I can't eat anything right now, and I don't think I'm ready to face my mother and Grandmother just yet," I answered.

"They're worried sick about you. I already let them
I heard from you and was on my way to pick you up,"
plied.

Sharon appeared very supportive, reassuring me that
was ready to stomp the devil's head with me. Actually she
to take some of the blame, feeling like there was some-
g she could have done. I quickly assured her this had
ing to do with her; this was entirely my fault.

"I didn't follow the suggestions of the N.A. Program. I
n't take heed to what Pastor had taught me and what I
w through the word of *God*. I wasn't truthful about my
counter with Dray, nor my thoughts of using. I didn't even
are the warning signs at my meetings. I wasn't honest with
yone, not even myself."

*elapse is never forced, nor is it even an accident. You have a
eservation; you have a choice.*

When we arrived back at the house, my family wel-
omed me with open arms. Even though in my mind I felt like
hey wanted to scold me, they didn't. They embraced me with
love, and I sincerely apologized, reassuring them I was well
on my way. The sign of not having that desire to use was one
of my many confirmations.

*Relapse can be the destruction force that kills us or leads us
to the realization of who and what we really are.*

I realized that in relapsing, there is no starting over.
You begin at the end; you begin at your bottom. Now I know
this first hand. I now know how important it is to share my
feeling of wanting to use, and that it's not abnormal, but it's
also important to remember that the desire to use will pass.
That's why the N.A. program suggests that the addict call
someone like a sponsor to discuss your feelings—that's when
the urge of using starts to pass, so you're able to gain relief.

My family and I continued to talk about what happened, my mother saying, "Baby I'm so glad you tried calling someone this time. That's when I knew you realized you made the wrong choice, and that wasn't your life anymore. Once you recognize that the Holy Spirit lives inside of you, you just can't take him anywhere; it won't feel right to you anymore."

"You're right mom. When I realized I put myself right back in a situation of selling my body again, all the past abuse replayed in my mind. I knew I couldn't go through that again! The voice inside of me told me to call on Jesus! And when I did, it gave me the strength to get out of there. He answered my call—I Thank You, Almighty Jesus Christ!"

You have persevered and have endured hardship for my name, and have not grown weary. Yet I hold this against you: You have forsaken your first love. Remember the height and do the things you did at first and repent. If you do not repent I will come to you and remove your lamp-stand from its place... But you have this in your favor...

Revelation 2:3-6

I went straight into my room to repent to the Lord...

"Lord I come to you as humble as I know how, asking you for forgiveness on this issue for the last time. I know what I did wrong and I'm ashamed for not standing on the word I so believe in or using the tools and knowledge you equipped me with, and provided for my life. I repent of any wrong doing, knowing and unknowingly. I ask that you continue to give me strength to face whatever it is to come. Lord, please continue to order my steps, as I brush myself off and get back up in this race. Lord, I'm not saying that I won't make mistakes, but it won't be this one. So as I lift you up to be the head of my life, I would be so ever grateful. I ask all this in your name Jesus, Amen!"

After relapsing, I still had a lot to do—there were several people to face. I went to my meetings letting them know I had used six days before receiving my one year anniversary chip in the fellowship. Of course they welcomed me back—the program is unconditional just like *God.*

That Sunday I stood before the church and shared my story of relapse and how when I called the name of Jesus, he was right there to see me through. I even told my parole officer, ready to accept all consequences. He assured me that it was "strike one," but there would be no strike two or three…I would be sent back to prison. I didn't worry about it much because I knew in my heart I was going to do all the things I needed to do to fight this disease, and my actions were going to be key.

My life moved forward from that point…I became an active member in my church by joining the usher board; I also started a meeting group called "Make a Choice to Rejoice", a meeting that was part of the Narcotics Anonymous Program with other recovering addicts at my church. I enrolled at the Michigan College of Beauty, graduating in 1990. As *God* started to bless me as a Hair Stylist, I was able to purchase my first home for Parisia and I, and my cup began to run over with some of the finer things in Life—even my own salon.

Newspaper Article written about my Company: Tanya Hair & Nails & Company

The biggest part of all, I continuously grew more and more in my word. I made a conscious decision not to use. And with *God* I took every day one day at a time. I chose not to hang around **people, places, or things** that didn't line up with the word of *God*. More importantly, I chose to listen to that inner voice we so freely call "Something." You know, "Something told me not to do it"…Well, I now know it's the "Holy Spirit" that lives inside of me. This journey of clean and sober living carries many warnings, but if you take the advice given and keep the communication open—it too shall pass… **"Just Don't Use"**

According to statistics, most addicts won't make it; they say "Once an addict, always an addict." But it's not true…Freedom from addiction can be guaranteed if sought after with dedicated determination, along with *God*.

I'm not saying there won't be struggles and challenges—many challenges are going to come your way, for example: children, spouses, family, health problems, bills to pay and decisions to make. Yet, the Word of God and the Twelve Steps (*even if you're not an addict*) in your everyday life can help you live life with "Freedom" from whatever ails you. It's also important that you exercise and practice your will to guard against your old behavior patterns that will try to creep back into your daily life…Remember…*"Faith without works is dead."*

Addiction is ongoing and still destroying people's lives. My all-time favorite, Whitney Houston, and many others have struggled all the way to the end with their addiction. There are many others still facing the disease of addiction as well. Let me leave you with this… "Failure takes place when we quit, when we give up and let the drug (or anything) control us. We as addicts have a responsibility to ourselves and to others to continue this journey through life *Clean and Sober*.

I could have died a thousand times over in those nine years of practicing as an addict, but by recognizing what I meant to *God* and his purpose for my life, he saw fit for me to live and tell this story...

Working the *God*-sent program called the "Twelve Steps" and sharing my testimony where ever I go, reminds me daily of where I've been, and at the same time I'm helping someone else. One of the many things I realize and can truly say today is all this has molded me into becoming the person I am, the person who I really love today and the person that wears no shame.

God had planned something better for me so that only to-gether with him I would be made perfect...

Hebrews 11:40

I and other addicts in recovery have already paid this price for you, so you and others never have to use...

But you dear friend build yourselves up in your most holy faith and pray in the Holy Spirit. Keep yourselves in GOD's love as you wait for the mercy of our Lord Jesus Christ to bring you eternal life. Be merciful to those who doubt. Snatch others from the fire and save them; to others show mercy, mixed with fear—hating even the clothing stained by cor-rupted Flesh. To him who is able to keep you from falling and to present to you before his glorious presence without fault and with great joy—to the only GOD our Savior be glory, majesty, power and authority, through Jesus Christ our Lord, before all ages, now and forevermore! Amen....

Jude 4:20-23

WHERE ARE THEY NOW?

- *Today Kim is 10+ years clean and sober; Mother of two and Grandmother.*

- *Tony is 6+ years clean and sober; Father of three and three grandchildren.*

- *Daryl is 16 years clean and sober; Father of four.*

- *Pastor Paris Lee Smith Sr.; Is still Ministering the Word of God.*

- *My daughter Parisia is Mother of three with her Bachelor's and Master's degrees in Social Work; She is a member of Delta Sigma Theta Sorority, Inc. and Eastern Star*

*These are just a few more testimonies of what our **Lord and Savior Jesus Christ** will do and if he did it for us, he certainly can do the same for you...**Just Try Him!!!***

RESEARCH

Cocaine is a central nervous system stimulant derived from the coca plant. In parts of South America, the leaves of the coca plant are chewed or brewed tea for their stimulant effects and prevent altitude sickness. Cocaine is also used medically in the United States as a topical anesthetic in nose and throat surgery.

Cocaine base, also known as **"Crack," "Ready rock," "Gravel," "Rock," or "Freebase"** All names you should be aware of...

Crack is heated in a pipe and its vapors are inhaled. Crack can also be dissolved and injected, but it's not as commonly injected as cocaine hydrochloride. The most common mixture is with heroin and known as **"Speedball."**

Side Effects:

· Reduces blood flow to the heart

· Causes serious irregularities in cardiac rhythm and can precipitate cardiac arrest

· Reduces blood flow to multiple regions of the brain

· Elevates blood pressure

· Increases the likelihood of stroke

· Produces bowel gangrene

· Other abdominal problems

Female Users: While cocaine use had declined overall, the drop in use is more apparent among males than females. Cocaine and Crack appears to maintain a stronghold among women, in many cities, more female than male arrestees test positive for cocaine. This is attributed, in large part to the phenomenon of trading sex for crack.

Cocaine use among Students reported: 1.3% of eight graders, 1.8% of tenth graders, and 2.6% of high school students and its current year's 6.7% seniors reported using cocaine. And also the new drug "Ecstasy" and "Molly" are drugs to watch out for.

WHY DO DRUG USERS DEVELOP CRAVINGS?

B ecause the neurochemical circuits of the brain define the rush as rewarding, they send out chemical messages urging the user to repeat the experience as soon as possible. With "Crack" the effects can wear off within ten minutes. After repeated use the peak high is accompanied by an equal and opposite low, characterized by fatigue, irritability, and dysphoria (the opposite of euphoria.)

Nonetheless the cravings to report the euphoria of the initial use persist. However, prolonged use of cocaine results in tolerance, which means the user has to make increasing amounts of the drug to receive the same desired effect. The user seeks out more frequent and larger doses to avoid the crash, but also trying to achieve the same initial rush—that you will never ever get again…

God, grant me the serenity to accept the things I cannot change, the courage to change the things I can, and the wisdom to know the difference…